SPORTS JOURNALISM

K.C. Thakur

CYBER TECH PUBLICATIONS
4264/3, Ansari Road, Daryaganj, New Delhi-110002 (India)
Ph.: 011-23244078, 011-43559448 Fax: 011-23280028
E-Mail: cyberpublicationsdelhi@yahoo.com
Website: www.cybertechpublications.com

SPORTS JOURNALISM

K.C. Thakur

First Edition **2025**

Published by :

G.S. Rawat for **Cyber Tech Publications**
4264/3, Ansari Road, Daryaganj, New Delhi-110002 (India)
Ph.: 011-23244078, 011-43559448 Fax: 011-23280028
E-Mail: cyberpublicationsdelhi@yahoo.com
Website: www.cybertechpublications.com

Printed at: Asian Offset Printers, Delhi-53

Preface

This Handbook covers the breadth of sports and media scholarship, one of the up-and-coming topics bridging media entertainment, sports management, and popular culture. Organized into historical, institutional, spectator, and critical studies perspectives, this volume brings together the work of many researchers into one quintessential volume, defining the full scope of the subject area. Editors Arthur Raney and Jennings Bryant have recruited contributors from around the world to identify and synthesize the research representing numerous facets of the sports-media relationship.

As a unique collection on a very timely topic, the volume offers chapters examining the development of sports media; production, coverage, and economics of sports media; sports media audiences; sports promotion; and race and gender issues in sports and media. Unique in its orientation and breadth, the Handbook of Sports and Media is destined to play a major role in the future development of this fast-growing area of study. It is a must-have work for scholars, researchers, and graduate students working in media entertainment, media psychology, mass media/mass communication, sports marketing and management, popular communication, popular culture, and cultural studies.

—*Author*

CONTENTS

1

Introduction

Sports journalism is a form of journalism that reports on sports topics and events. While the sports department within some newspapers has been mockingly called the *toy department*, because sports journalists do not concern themselves with the 'serious' topics covered by the news desk, sports coverage has grown in importance as sport has grown in wealth, power and influence.

Sports journalism is an essential element of any news media organization. Sports journalism includes organizations devoted entirely to sports reporting — newspapers such as *L'Equipe* in France, *La Gazzetta dello Sport* in Italy, *Marca* in Spain, and the now defunct *Sporting Life* in Britain, American magazines such as *Sports Illustrated* and the *Sporting News*, all-sports talk radio stations, and television networks such as Eurosport, ESPN and The Sports Network (TSN).

SPORTS JOURNALISTS' ACCESS

Sports teams are not always very accommodating to journalists: in the United States, while they allow reporters into locker rooms for interviews and some extra information, sports teams provide extensive information support, even if reporting it is unfavorable to them.

Elsewhere in the world, particularly in the coverage of soccer, the journalist's role is often barely tolerated by the clubs and players.

For example, despite contractual media requirements in the English Premier League, prominent managers Sir Alex Ferguson (of Manchester United) and Harry Redknapp (first at Portsmouth, now at Tottenham) have refused to conduct post-match interviews with the BBC because of unfavorable coverage by the television channel's news department.

As with reporters on other news beats, sports journalism involves investigating the story, rather than simply relying on press releases and prepared statements from the sports team, coaching staff, or players. Sports journalists verify facts given to them by the athletes, teams, leagues, or organizations they are covering.

Access for sports journalists is usually easier for north American professional and intercollegiate sports such as football, ice hockey, basketball and baseball where the commercial relationship between media coverage and increased ticket, merchandise, or advertising sales, is better understood.

SOCIO-POLITICAL SIGNIFICANCE

Major League Baseball gave print journalists a special role in its games: They were named official scorers and kept statistics that were considered part of the official record of the league. Active sportswriters were removed from this role in 1980. Although their statistical judgment calls could not affect the outcome of a game in progress, the awarding of errors and wins/saves were seen as powerful influences on pitching staff selections and play lists when coach decisions seemed unusual. The removal of writers, who could benefit fiscally from sensational sports stories, was done to remove this perception of a conflict of interest, and to increase statistics volume, consistency, and accuracy.

Sports stories occasionally transcend the games themselves and take on socio-political significance: Jackie Robinson breaking the color barrier in baseball is an example of this. Modern controversies regarding the hyper-compensation of top athletes, the use of anabolic steroids and other, banned performance-enhancing drugs, and the cost to local and national governments to build sports venues and related infrastructure, especially for Olympic Games, also demonstrate how sports intrudes on to the news pages.

Sportswriters regularly face more deadline pressure than other reporters because sporting events tend to occur late in the day and closer to the deadlines many organizations must observe. Yet they are expected to use the same tools as news journalists, and to uphold the same professional and ethical standards. They must take care not to show bias for any team.

Many of the most talented and respected print journalists have been sportswriters.

SPORTS JOURNALISM IN EUROPE

The tradition of sports reporting attracting some of the finest writers in journalism can be traced to the coverage of sport in Victorian England, where several modern sports - such as association football, cricket, athletics and rugby - were first organized and codified into something resembling what we would recognize today.

Cricket, somewhat like baseball in the United States, possibly because of its esteemed place in society, has regularly attracted the most elegant of writers.

The *Manchester Guardian*, in the first half of the 20th Century, employed Neville Cardus as its cricket correspondent as well as its music critic. Cardus was later knighted for his services to journalism. One of his successors, John Arlott, who became a worldwide favorite because of his radio commentaries on the BBC, and was also known for his poetry.

The first London Olympic Games in 1908 attracted such widespread public interest that many newspapers assigned their very best-known writers to the event. The *Daily Mail* even had Sir Arthur Conan Doyle at the White City Stadium to cover the finish of the first ever 26-mile, 385-yard Marathon.

Such was the drama of that race, in which Dorando Pietri collapsed within sight of the finishing line when leading, that Conan Doyle led a public subscription campaign to see the gallant Italian, having been denied the gold medal through his disqualification, awarded a special silver cup, which was presented by Queen Alexandra.

And the public imagination was so well caught by the event that annual races in Boston, Ma, and London, and at future Olympics, were henceforward staged over exactly the same, 26-mile, 385-yard distance, the official length of the event worldwide to this day.

The London race, called the Polytechnic Marathon and originally staged over the 1908 Olympic route from outside the royal residence at Windsor Castle to White City, was first sponsored by the *Sporting Life*, which in those Edwardian times was a daily newspaper which sought to cover all sporting events, rather than just a betting paper for horse racing and greyhounds that it became in the years after the Second World War.

In France, *L'Auto*, the predecessor of *L'Equipe*, had already played an equally influential part in the sporting fabric of society when it announced in 1903 that it would stage an annual bicycle race around the country. The Tour de France was born, and sports journalism's role in its foundation is still reflected today in the leading rider wearing a yellow jersey - the color of the paper on which *L'Auto* was published (in Italy, the Giro d'Italia established a similar tradition, with the leading rider wearing a jersey the same pink color as the sponsoring newspaper, *La Gazzetta*).

SPORTS STARS IN THE PRESS BOX

After the Second World War, the sports sections of British national daily and Sunday newspapers continued to expand, to the point where many papers now have separate standalone sports sections; some Sunday tabloids even have sections, additional to the sports pages, devoted solely to the previous day's football reports. In some respects, this has replaced the earlier practice of many regional newspapers which - until overtaken by the pace of modern electronic media - would produce special results editions rushed out on Saturday evenings.

Some newspapers, such as the *The Sunday Times*, with 1924 Olympic 100 m champion Harold Abrahams, or the London *Evening News* using former England cricket captain Sir Leonard Hutton, began to adopt the policy of hiring former sports stars to pen columns, which were often ghost written. Some such ghosted columns, however, did little to further the reputation of sports journalism, which is increasingly becoming the subject of academic scrutiny of its standards.

Many "ghosted" columns were often run by independent sports agencies, based in Fleet Street or in the provinces, who had signed up the sports star to a contract and then syndicated their material among various titles. These agencies included Pardons, or the Cricket Reporting Agency, which routinely provided the editors of the Wisden cricket almanac, and Hayters (now known as Infostrada Hayters).

Sportswriting in Britain has attracted some of the finest journalistic talents. The *Daily Mirror*'s Peter Wilson, Hugh McIlvanney, first at *The Observer* and lately at the *Sunday Times*, Ian Wooldridge of the *Daily Mail* and soccer writer Brian Glanville, best known at the *Sunday Times*, and columnist Patrick Collins, of the *Mail on Sunday*, five times the winner of the Sports Writer of the Year Award.

Many became household names in the late 20th Century through their trenchant reporting of often earth-shattering events that have transcended the back pages and been reported on the front pages: the Massacre at the Munich Olympics in 1972; Muhammad Ali's fight career, including his 1974 title bout against George Foreman; the Heysel Stadium disaster; and the career highs and lows of the likes of George Best and Lester Piggott and other high profile stars.

McIlvanney and Wooldridge, who died in March 2007, aged 75, both enjoyed careers that saw them frequently work in television.

During his career, Wooldridge became so famous that, like the sports stars he reported upon, he hired the services of IMG, the agency founded by the American businessman, Mark McCormack, to manage his affairs. And Glanville wrote several books, including novels, as well as scripting the memorable official film to the 1966 World Cup staged in England.

SPECIALIST SPORTS AGENCIES

The 1950s and 1960s saw a rapid growth in sports coverage, both in print and on broadcast media. It also saw the development of specialist sports news and photographic agencies. For example, photographer Tony Duffy founded the picture agency AllSport in south London shortly after the 1964 Tokyo Olympics, and, through some outstanding photography (such as Duffy's iconic image of the American long jumper Bob Beamon flying through the air towards his world record at the 1968 Mexico City Olympics) and the astute marketing of its images, saw the business grow into a multi-million pound, worldwide concern that ultimately would be bought and re-named Getty Images.

SPORTS BOOKS

Increasingly, sports journalists have turned to long-form writing, producing popular books on a range of sporting topics, including biographies, history and investigations.

In London, through the 1980s and 1990s, one shop on Charing Cross Road - the area known for its book shops - was entirely devoted to sport, although the growth of online book sales through websites such as Amazon eventually led to the closure of Sports Books.

This was not before, though, the establishment, through sponsorship from William Hill, the bookmakers, of an annual prize for the sports book of the year. This was first held in 1989, when Dan Topolski's book about one of the most controversial University Boat Races was declared the winner.

The status of the awards, and of sports books generally, were enhanced greatly in 1992 when Nick Hornby's first novel, *Fever Pitch*, took first prize. Both *Fever Pitch* and *True Blue: The Oxford Boat Race Mutiny* have subsequently been adapted into feature-length motion pictures. Only one author, Donald McRae, in 1996 and 2002, has won the William Hill award more than once.

Unsurprisingly, given cricket writers' often literary aspirations and the appetite for books on cricket, the summer game has four times been the subject of the prize-winning book, the same number as football.

The award has not been without controversy in recent years. In 2000, the award went for the first time to a "ghosted" book, Lance Armstrong's *It's Not About the Bike*. At the time, some also observed the irony of the award going to the American Tour de France winner, when, in 1990, Paul Kimmage's stern critique of doping in cycling, *Rough Ride*, had been declared the winner.

The judges - the same panel is used each year - were also criticised in 2006 when they chose Geoffrey Ward's *Unforgivable Blackness*, because it had been first published in 2004.

The 2007 winner of the award, announced at a ceremony staged at Waterstones, Piccadilly, on November 27, was *Provided You Don't Kiss Me*, the account of local newspaper reporter Duncan Hamilton working with the controversial Nottingham Forest manager, Brian Clough.

Winners of the William Hill Sports Book of the Year

2008: *Coming Back To Me*, Marcus Trescothick (with Peter Hayter)

2007: *Provided You Don't Kiss Me*, Duncan Hamilton

2006: *Unforgivable Blackness*, Geoffrey Ward

2005: *My Father and other Working Football Class Heroes*, Gary Imlach

2004: *Basil D'Oliveira*, Peter Oborne

2003: *Broken Dreams*, Tom Bower

2002: *In Black & White*, Donald McRae

2001: *Seabiscuit - The True Story Of 3 Men & A Race Horse*, Laura Hillenbrand

2000: *It's Not About the Bike - My Journey Back to Life*, Lance Armstrong

1999: *A Social History of English Cricket*, Derek Birley

1998: *Angry White Pyjamas*, Robert Twigger

1997: *A Lot Of Hard Yakka*, Simon Hughes

1996: *Dark Trade*, Donald McRae

1995: *A Good Walk Spoiled*, John Feinstein

1994: *Football Against The Enemy*, Simon Kuper

1993: *Endless Winter*, Stephen Jones

1992: *Fever Pitch*, Nick Hornby

1991: *Muhammad Ali: His Life and Times*, Thomas Hauser

1990: *Rough Ride*, Paul Kimmage

1989: *True Blue*, Dan Topolski

INVESTIGATIVE JOURNALISM AND SPORT

Since the 1990s, the growing importance of sport, its impact as a global business and the huge amounts of money involved from sponsorship and in the staging of the Olympic Games and football World Cups, has also attracted the attention of well-known investigative journalists.

The sensitive nature of the relationships between sports journalists and the subjects of their reporting, as well as declining budgets experienced by most Fleet Street newspapers, has meant that such long-term projects have often emanated from television documentary makers.

Tom Bower, with his 2003 sports book of the year *Broken Dreams*, which analyzed British football, followed in the tradition established a decade earlier by Andrew Jennings and Vyv Simson with their controversial investigation of corruption within the International Olympic Committee. Jennings and Simson's *The Lords of the Rings* in many ways predicted the scandals that were to emerge around the staging of the 2002 Winter Olympics in Salt Lake City; Jennings would follow-up with two further books on the Olympics and one on FIFA, the world football body. Likewise, award-winning writers Duncan Mackay, of *The Guardian*, and Steven Downes unravelled many scandals involving doping, fixed races and bribery in international athletics in their 1996 book, *Running Scared*, which offered an account of the threats by a senior track official that led to the suicide of their sports journalist colleague, Cliff Temple.

But the writing of such exposes - referred to as "spitting in the soup" by Paul Kimmage, the former Tour de France professional cyclist, who now writes for the *Sunday Times* - often requires the view of an outsider who is not compromised by the need of day-to-day dealings with sportsmen and officials, as required by "beat" correspondents.

The stakes can be high when upsetting sport's powers: when in 2007, the English FA opted to switch its multi-million pound contract for UK coverage rights of the FA Cup and England international matches from the BBC to rival broadcasters ITV, one of the reasons cited was that the BBC had been too critical of the performances of the England football team.

SPORTS JOURNALISM ORGANIZATIONS

Most countries have their own national association of sports journalists. Many sports also have their own clubs and associations for specialist journalists. These organizations tend not to operate as trades unions, but do attempt to maintain the standard of press provision at sports venues, oversee fair accreditation procedures and to celebrate high standards of sports journalism.

In Britain, the Sports Journalists' Association was founded in 1948. It stages two prestigious awards events, an annual Sports Awards ceremony which recognises outstanding performances by British sportsmen and women during the previous year, and the British Sports Journalism Awards, the industry's "Oscars", sponsored by UK Sport and presented each March.

Originally founded as the Sports Writers' Association, following a merger with the Professional Sports Photographers' Association in 2002 the organization changed its title to the more inclusive SJA.

Its President is the veteran broadcaster and columnist, Sir Michael Parkinson.

The SJA represents the British sports media on the British Olympic Association's press advisory committee and acts as a consultant to organizers of major events who need guidance on media requirements as well as seeking to represent its members' interests in a range of activities.

In March 2008, Martin Samuel, then the chief football correspondent of *The Times*, was named British Sportswriter of the Year, the first time any journalist had managed to win the award three years in succession.

At the same awards, Jeff Stelling, of Sky Sports, was named Sports Broadcaster of the Year for the third time, a prize determined by a ballot of SJA members. Stelling won the vote again the following year, when the *Sunday Times*'s Paul Kimmage won the interviewer of the year prize for a fifth time.

The International Sports Press Association, AIPS, was founded in 1924 during the Olympic Games in Paris, at the headquarters of the Sporting Club de France, by Frantz Reichel, the press chief of the Paris Games, and the Belgian, Victor Boin.

The first statutes of AIPS mentioned these objectives:

- to enhance the cooperation between its member associations in defending sport and the professional interest of their members.

- to strengthen the friendship, solidarity and common interests between sports journalists of all countries.
- to assure the best possible working conditions for the members.

AIPS operates through a system of continental sub-associations and national associations, and liaises closely with some of the world's biggest sports federations, including the International Olympic Committee, FIFA, football's world governing body and the IAAF, the international track and field body.

FANZINES AND BLOGS

Through the 1970s and '80s, a rise in "citizen journalism" in Europe was witnessed in the rapid growth in popularity of soccer "fanzines" - cheaply printed magazines written by fans for fans that bypassed often stilted official club match programs and traditional media. Many continue today and thrive. Some authors have been adopted by their clubs - Jim Munro, once editor of the West Ham United fanzine *Fortune's Always Dreaming*, was hired by the club to write for its matchday magazine and is now sports editor of The Sun Online. Other titles, such as the irreverent monthly soccer magazine *When Saturday Comes*, have effectively gone mainstream.

The advent of the internet has seen much of this fan-generated energy directed into sports blogs. Ranging from team-centric blogs to those that cover the sports media itself, Deadspin.com, ProFootballTalk.com, AOL Fanhouse, the blogs in the Yardbarker Network, and others have garnered massive followings.

Blogging has also been taken up by sportsmen and women such as Curt Schilling, Paula Radcliffe, Greg Oden, Donovan McNabb, and Chris Cooley.

How objective is our journalism?

We, as sports journalists, stand accused of complicity by the latest issue of the *British Journalism Review*. We are said to be witting parties to turning what ought to be objective reporting into little more than advertorials draped around the odd football match or track meeting.

"News is what someone wants to suppress. Everything else is advertising," was the view of Rubin Frank of NBC.

I was reminded of that again the other day when the phone in Downes Mansions rang, and a very pleasant young woman from a PR agency was on the line. There's an international championship coming up, and the new sponsors of this particular sport in Britain wanted to send me to the event.

All flights and hotel costs (and a very nice hotel, too) would be looked after, and there was even an invitiation to dinner with the sponsors' chief executive before the event began. All I'd have to do is to get a couple of reports on the event into print, maybe do a radio two-way as well. The newspapers and radio stations would pay me, I'd have no costs, and at no point did the PR mention whether "the client" expected to get a mention. A freelancer's nirvana. What's a boy to do?

Say "no" might be the simple answer. But would it do any good? There was one esteemed colleague who steadfastly refused ever to accept the various dodgy T-shirts doled out to us hacks at accreditation desks around the world. But still the T-shirts keep coming. And what sports journalist has never supped with the devil, or at least had a glass of chilled Chablis provided with some food at an event at the sponsor's expense?

Too much "top-level", professional sport these days is staged less out of any true competitive purpose, but simply to deliver some extra airtime for the sponsors.

The recent, two-day athletics international in Birmingham was one case in point: the event was organised without, according to one senior national coach, any proper reference to UK Athletics' performance department. The marketeers needed to fulfil TV and sponsor obligations. But how many athletics writers hedged their reports with a "health warning" for their readers that the event was little more than a circus performance, rather than *real* sport?

Eamon Dunphy, the former Irish football international turned outspoken pundit, rails against what he has called the "soft consensus" in sports reporting, something which Professor Raymond Boyle, in an article in the latest edition of the *British Journalism Review* describes thus:

> Much of what passes for journalism in British television coverage of football exists within an all-too-cosy network of ex-players and current managers. The few journalists involved seem unprepared to risk upsetting this closed world by asking difficult questions.

Professor Boyle, a career academic based at Stirling, warms to his theme as he turns to newspapers' short-comings on their sports pages, too: "In the increasingly overtly commercial world of media sport, largely anodyne interviews in the sports, features or magazine pages of the print media often appear to be adverts for a range of endorsed products.

"Secure an interview with Michael Owen, but make sure some explicit references to the sponsor organising access, such as Tissot watches, appears in the piece... Within these constraints even the most experienced of journalist can struggle to turn a turgid PR-staged interview into anything remotely insightful."

Prof Boyle cites the examples of World Cup "columnists" Alan Shearer and Geoff Hurst, pictured, whose copy was bought and paid for by Continental Tyres and McDonald's, respectively. In these days of ever-tightening budgets, such cheap, or even free, "star name" copy is embraced eagerly. But how often does it actually deliver anything of real value to the reader?

The compromise goes further. Take the pundits in the BBC and ITV studios: was Shearer or Terry Venables ever likely to be overtly critical of the England team's performances in Germany when both were being courted at around that time for a job with the post-Eriksson coaching staff?

"Framed by entertainment rather than journalistic values and with too many vested interests involved, football coverage on television tends now to be driven by soft opinion rather than hard analysis. Television often appears to see its role as promoting sport, rather than reporting, investigating and analysing," says Prof Boyle.

Football is not alone. The "soft consensus" was found last week in the cricket press box, effectively neutering the coverage of that sport's latest crisis. How could Michael Atherton (dirt in pocket) or Derek Pringle (pictured, who admitted his own ball tampering when playing) possibly take the moral high ground against Pakistan?

And what of the valued opinions of the man who once described Pakistan as "the kind of place to send your mother-in-law for a month, all expenses paid"? Ian Botham's legal track record, following his lost libel case against Imran Khan, may well have had an influence on his analysis of the situation at the Oval Test.

As Prof Boyle says in his *BJR* article: "Too many journalists and former sports people abdicate their responsibility to report honestly because they may upset important people or damage their own career trajectory."

But this is about much more than the old hack's complaint against former pros who stroll straight from dressing room to press box. For now, with increasing pressures on sports desk budgets and ever-diminishing returns for freelancers, there is a growing trend for journalsts to be paid for.

It is a practice that has been prevelant on business, fashion, motoring and travel desks for decades: PRs offering attractive foreign trips, in return for some tailored copy a few weeks down the line. *The Independent*, at its launch in the 1980s, took the high moral ground in banning all such "freebies".

But elsewhere in journalism, the practice is so widespread as to be almost unavoidable. Reuters, the international news agency, applies a high-minded "no freebies" policy for its own staff; however, if freelancers are paid by a sponsor to attend an event, it has tended to turn a blind eye, take their copy and pay its stringer its modest lineage rate.

And herewith comes the *mea culpa*: earlier this month, I covered the European athletics championships at the expense of the local organisers. Together with three colleagues, we were paid to provide an agency news service on the meeting, which appeared on the event's website and in the press centre. Hand on heart, I never once wrote a sponsor's name into my copy.

There are some sports events, and their faithful sponsors, that are so starved of mainstream exposure in pages or on channels dominated by football, that they are increasingly directing their marketing spends towards sports journalists and television producers.

One non-Olympic sport governing body recently paid all the TV production costs for a series of international matches, in order to *give* the resulting footage to a terrestrial channel, and thus ensure its sponsors got the coverage they crave. No where in the broadcast programme was any caveat mentioned that "this segment is brought to you by Sudsy Suds".

Yet this insidious, sponsor-satisfying technique is spreading ever further, to the perhaps esoteric pages of your local newspaper, and even to a professional sportswriters' organisation near you.

For the specialist writers of one major Olympic sport have arranged to have their annual awards dinner sponsored and organised by the marketing agents and self-same major sponsor of the sport which they are supposed to be observing objectively throughout the year.

And one "news" agency is now shamelessly plugging its own subscription to the "soft consensus".

The agency's website reports that its "coverage of major athletics events in 2006 will be supported by Norwich Union".

"Supported"? By the insurance company that is pumping millions into the very sport that this agency is supposed to be reporting on objectively?

The shameless admission on the news agency's website continues: "Copy provided to the agency's network of regional press titles will be branded to reflect Norwich Union's £50 million six-year commitment to UK Athletics... The service will be available...and sports editors will be able to take advantage of preview and live copy, free of charge." But at what price?

We will be discussing how to create feature stories with video. Your role is that of a journalist, and your job is to write a story for the event. The story you write will make the footage come alive for the viewer. The story will be the emphasis, which may help your team or a specific player become great. You may be having your own cameraperson and/or you may be using the footage from the game camera. You as a reporter should remember this about your game-camera or sideline videographer.

Their job is to capture the action, and during the game the framing of the shots and keeping up with the action will be what they are thinking about. Oftentimes they will not be able to tell you what the game was actually like. Shooting the game is a specialized and difficult process, it is telling the story visually, and this person is continuously working and keeping a good picture for the entire event. They only see through the viewfinder, and miss much of the story, Do not rely on them to write your story - rather your story and their visual story is one which you will work together on in editing and create your feature.

However if you are going to create feature stories about sports you will have to know how to put together a good story. There is not much of a leap from a print story to a video story. But to make that leap you are going to have to learn to write.

You have the regular Television News story that is 30 seconds or less and you have a feature story, which may be any length. We will discuss the longer feature here rather than the short clip. While you are in the reporter mode try and forget that you are making a video feature, pretend that your words alone will have to tell the entire story. In this way the addition of the video will make your story stand out.

You are used to going to the games and talking about them afterwards, you can expand your short versions to a real story. We are going to put together a plan here.

Introduce yourself, as a reporter you need to identify your self to everyone you will need to speak with. Have a nice card printed, (with the computer available you can print your own card) preferably one that has your picture on it. Few people have their photo on a card, this alone will help you stand out in the mind of the people you will be working with. Introductions are important for the remainder of the season, the first introduction will be the one remembered so make the best impression you can - even dress up and wear a tie for a change - **Laughing**

1. Going to the game is the first thing, your job starts well before the game because there is a lot of information you need to have. Before the game is time you will have to get it. You will need the rosters for both teams and the statistics for both teams. You want the coach's names. You want the schedules. The statistics are important but they are not the entire story, you use them to make the story more interesting. Do not rely on statistics to write the story for you. Get all the newspapers the next day and clip (cut out) the stories that were written, add these to the information which you gather during the game. Reading these stories will often add to the story which you write, If you do use any of this material - give the reporter and the paper credit - the last thing you want is to make an enemy of a fellow reporter or the paper they work for. Other reporters are excellent

sources of information and a comradrary and friend ship exists between all of the reporters and photographers of the different media. Be free with what you know and share, help the other members of the working press as much as possible. This is really the spirit of reporting. A simple thing is to have a multiple power connector to plug in your electronics, and share the extra plugs with other reporters. Duplicate mikes, headsets, and other cords are good for you but will allow you to be a good person to know at the games, pencils, papers, scotch-tape and duct-tape, extra copies of the rosters and the statistics are good to have to share.

2. Get all of the background interviews before the game, after the game you will get the reactions to the outcome. If you are doing an unbiased version you will have interviews from both teams, if your doing a piece for your team and being supportive you will only interview your players.
3. You don't get to just watch the game - you have to keep the statistics and write the story as you go, make notes and be creative.
4. After the game you get your final interviews with the heroes and coaches, or any other special interest story you are working on.
5. Now the real work takes place you have to set down and write your story. Write as much as you possibly can, the big stores and the little ones. You have your heroes but you have the other heroes who seldom get recognized - the player's assists are what make heroes. The way the team works together is what results in a winning team. Your viewpoint will be special and the more comprehensive and complete you are the better the story. Your stories can help make a team and can definitely make a player.
6. Think you're done - nope - now go back and re-read it and revise it. Clean it up.

7. Done yet - nope - now read the story OUTLOUD - with PACEING AND EMOTION - how does it sound - is the sentence structure clear - now you need to go back and make it HEARABLE AND UNDERSTANDABLE for the viewers.
8. The final step is the voice over itself - and - as you read it for the recording you will undoubtedly want to change a word or two - but try to keep this to a minimum, writing the story over as you record it will take you forever and you really don't have that much time.
9. You will have a mix of audio for the final program –
   - Natural sound from the game
   - The interviews
   - Your commentary
   - Music and or sound effects
   - A feature program is not simply the reading of your story it is the compilation of all the parts of the documentation process.

NOW WHAT DO YOU HAVE

The Beginning of Your Video Script

We are not finished with the discussion of writing yet. How we will expand your story into a video program will come later. I just wanted to make the point now.

You story is going to be viewed well after the event is over, and this can be a real plus for you. You have reported the story and you have the writing and the revision done, now you can go back once more and get the inside story. Expand the story into a timeless piece.

The coverage of the team will be a long-term project and over the course of the season you are going to gather many unrelated facts and stores, a good notebook or system of files is going to be indispensable for you now. As you write the story your research and will come together and you can tie things which you did not believe you would use into an interesting and complete story.

Now back to the beginning again, before the event. You need to know the rules, if you are going to understand the calls of the referees. And if you know the rules you can comment on the game in a more complete manner.

A knowledge of the rules of a game and the knowledge of the game itself is not static - the game changes - the rules change - the style of playing changes. You as a sports writer/videographer will need to know and keep up with the sport, and not just one sport but all of the ones you cover.

There are a number of people that you need to know, the principal, and the athletic director, all of the coaches, players, managers, and business manager. All of these people are sources of information for you, and you will need to speak with them all at one time or the other.

Quotes - get used to making the quotes in context, and are absolutely accurate. The video camera is going to be indispensable for you here, because you don't have to transcribe the words.

Your questions will determine how freely the person talks, you will want to spend a few minutes with each person you interview and discuss what you are going to ask them, so they can get the topics in their mind. If you have prepared before the game you can have the questions written out. and give the list to them before the game, when you ask them if you may come to them after the game for the interview.

Examples of the List

Interviewer - "This is Coach (name) of the V/JV/S - M/W (sport) team"((complement the team))

1. "Coach (you had a good/rough game today/tonight) ??How would you describe the overall flow of the game??

2. "Coach on offense you have some good players, tell me about 3 different players which earned comment this game.
3. same question - defense -
4. was there a key play, which made the game a win for you
5. Player (name) was injured today/tonight how are they now?
6. Player (names) injured in the past how are they - will they come back?
7. (the next game is always one to worry about) Coach we play (name) next, what preparation are you planning for the practices? What are the strengths of that team?
8. Coach tell me about the entire season and how you project the rest of the season.

In editing you will cut some of the comments, and cover them with action or still shots. Don't hurry the person you are interviewing - and don't cut them short so you can get to the next question. Sometimes the person will ramble and take a while to get to the point, its alright. You will be able to have more material to edit (choose from) Hopefully the interview will be so smooth that you will be able to use all of it.

PLAYER INTERVIEWS - you will want to make these interviews - and get the responses and feelings of the player - their history - Practice sessions and after the game -are the best times - If you are going to do pre-game interviews do them well before the game starts, a couple of hours if possible.

Team Group shots

Is there a sports expert - (student)(parent)(fan) who you can interview - ?

INFORMATION DURING THE GAME

You will need to learn to organize your self and have the method for saving all of your information. Things you will need

1. A clipboard and plenty of paper. If you are doing play by play have two clip boards (or a stiff cardboard which you can have two papers side by side)and tape so you can secure the rosters
2. Blank the statistics sheets
3. extra pencils and a small sharpener
4. A steno pad
5. A couple of large zip lock plastic bags to store materials, you can use these to put notes into as you compete sections - the program - and other materials which you will gather. I recommend large zip-lock bags because they are waterproof - and can be the file folder for the information later on - these bags will keep the pages from becoming scattered.

A waterproof marker will be handy to write on the outside of the bag for later identification.

Conference games - may have the managers print the statistics and distribute them to the reporters at half-time and following the game - be sure to pick up these copies. The school paper is a good source of information - if one is available put one of them in the bag also.

You don't have to set in the press box that little table may end up being more of a problem than an asset. Place yourself where you have another point of view, such as behind the players bench, or in the crowd. You will see and hear the game differently from another point.

The attitude of the crowd and what they say may give you a better story. If your are behind the scorers table you will be able to follow the discussions, which always happen during a game. These are little vignettes, which can be good for your story.

If you are doubling as a cameraperson, while writing these stories you will not be shooting continuously. Instead you will only shoot when some particular event occurs. Also if you are responsible for the interviews after the game - your nearness to the court will place you in a position to reach the Players - Coaches - or Officials faster. After the game there is always a press of people trying to speak with all of them. Being there first will give you the best chance of having your questions answered. In this situation the camera will be hand held or preferably on a monopod - Stable shots are important.

The reporter & photographer team — this is the best way to get the interviews. Now from the start remember you are a team - and you help each other - setting up and carrying equipment - contacting people and gathering information -

If you observe the professional television news teams, you will see this is not the case, rather the reporter (on camera personality) will more likely have an elitist attitude - If you are the Reporter don't start you career as a prima-donna, you will make your photographer hate you, and the other media personnel will laugh at you. Again I am stressing the importance of the team attitude, you may be the star but you won't be for long unless you strive to be helpful and share the workload.

This manual being written to give you the tools to become a true professional, and if not a professional to produce really great amateur videos.

Using the camera as both a way of recording the action and reporting the game makes an interesting technique. You can shoot the action and following or during the shot make a comment on the tape. Your on camera mike will pick up your voice well - if the game is loud - speak up - a little experimentation will give you the knowledge of how loud you need to be. You can have a headset mike plugged into the camera for this purpose.

You have four options when recording into the camera

1. the on camera microphone
2. A hard-wired mike - Be sure to have a good insulated cable to connect between the mike and the camera. (here you have the option of a hand held mike or a lavaliere (clip-on) mike

3. A wireless (hand held or clip on) mike and receiver
4. the facility may have an audio breakout box

Each one of these options will require you to have a different technique when you shoot, and interview.

(1.) you will need to be close to the subject and have your camera zoomed out wide;

(2.) Being hardwired, you can be further away - the mike may be placed on a podium or clipped on the subject.

(3.) Wireless - you are going to be subject to many variables, it is a good thing to have a receiver which you can tune to the house frequency- your own mike frequency may be interfered with by - cell phones - short wave - CB - am/fm radio - television station - other wireless mikes - transformers - electrical cabling - microwave transmitters - or the battery may just die - The wireless mikes are the most subject to problems of all - be ready to change to another system.

(4.) The Breakout box, is a box, which the house will provide to the video crews, to keep the podiums from being filled with microphones, and the floor covered with cabling. - these boxes have XLR connections and you may have a MINI PLUG on your camera. be ready to adapt. Have a long XLR cable for this connection. An adapter to go from XLR to MINI.

The choice of HAND-HOLDING - MONO-POD - TRIPOD holding of the camera will depend on the circumstances. If you are using a new lightweight camera you need some kind of support, or the camera will be shaking all over the place. You can use your tripod as a monopod by extending just one leg, have the head loose and support and direct it with both hands. A monopod is better than shoulder holding the camera but not as good as using the tripod for stability. Refer to the page on FIELD and look at the list of possible shots which your photographer will be finding from the sideline positions. These shots are all elements of your story, and you need to be aware of what is going on every where as a reporter - not just the action on the field.

We have gotten all the way to here, and have not talked about the editing of the video.

The question now, do you have to fit into a time frame or can this feature be of any length. It will be best to work in 10 min, 15-min -30-min - one hour time frames. Now depending on the nature of the story and the material you have available you will pick one of those time frames. I'm not locking the time in stone its just a guide line.

the times you will add up to determine the program length will be:

1. Your Story as a voice over. covered with video
2. your interviews - a mix of subject and illustrative video
3. the Cutaways with crowd sideline comments
4. game footage - with or without play by play - and or natural sound
5. the time for the title and introduction
6. the time for the close and the credits.

Your story is going to determine how the video footage is used, and so you will record your story piece by piece - remember - the phrases, sentences and paragraphs will have footage to illustrate both covering the speaker and \ between the speeches.

List all of the shots/scenes in categories, shots for the - open - interviews - game camera footage - floor camera game footage - cutaways - close footage.

In vision - your video starts with an open - a set of scenes and title screens, you will have either music or natural sounds over this section.

This section may fade to black and fade to the introduction

How do you introduce the video, your choice - a voice over or shot of the narrator

from your introduction you assemble your program with all of the narrative sections, you will go back and insert video to cover the black.

If you have your voice over sections with a black screen as the video or the narrator as a talking head - It will be clear where your inserts belong.

The inserting of the footage is a creative process, and you will probably make changes as you insert edit. Commonly you will shorten up the existing cutaways and add more shots, to pick up the pacing of the program.

As you look at the project, most likely you will have a stack of tapes and a lot of sheets of paper.

Your Editing script will have the TAPE NUMBER AND THE TIME CODE OR CONTROL TRACK NUMBER LISTED

Remember to log the tape well - have the tape clearly labeled and the accompanying log labeled and keep them close. if there is time-code on your tape finding a specific clip will be much easier, because they are always present. If you are relying on control track numbers the tape will have to be rewound each time and the counter zeroed for you to find the clip. The DIGITAL format has the time code numbers - usually the VHS, SVHS, 8mm, and Hi8, do not have them.

After you have edited a few programs you will develop your own system and style. However you list and mark your tapes and information makes it consistent and clear. You will find yourself making last minute changes, correcting and improving the program. In spite of your best effort to be accurate, you will find many times the information you were given is wrong, or has changed, you will want to correct all of the mistakes, and if you cannot find the clips you need you will have to spend a lot of extra time.

2

The Art of the Interview

Being an exceptional sports writer simply means being an exceptional interviewer— the writing pales if the interviewing skills are mediocre. You can't use in print what you don't get during an interview.

Some techniques are simply timeless. Consider the following three quotations, the first from William Zinsser (1985) book, *On Writing Well, An Informal Guide to Writing Nonfiction*; the second is from John Brady (1976) *The Craft of Inter- viewing*; and the last is from DeWitt Reddick (1949) *Modern Feature Writing*.

These guidelines are as important today as when they were first published:

Interviewing is one of those skills that you only get better at. You will never again feel so ill at ease as when you try for the first time, and probably you will never feel entirely comfortable prodding another person for answers that he or she may be too shy to reveal, or too inarticulate. But at least half of the skill is purely mechanical.

The rest is instinct—knowing how to make the other person relax, when to push, when to listen, when to stop. And this can be learned with experience. (Zinsser, 1985, p. 79)

Interviewing is the modest, immediate science of gaining trust, then gaining information. Both ends must be balanced if the interview is to be balanced and incisive. Yet they are often fumbled in the anxious heat of an interview. The interviewer will either yearn too desperately for his subject's trust and evoke flatulence, or he will restrain his sympathies, demand data—and get like in return.

The writer should prepare in advance many of the questions he plans to ask. These questions should not be haphazard and unrelated, but should spring from the central idea of the story, as he sees it. Preferably he should visualize two or three possible lines of development for the story, and think out questions along each line; thus he will be prepared to adjust himself to the line which seems most promising during the interview. The beginner will find it helpful to write out his leading questions; most experienced writers may prefer to think clearly through the story as it may develop along three or four angles, and to carry these lines of thought in mind.

There are a variety of techniques and tricks of the trade regarding the *art* and *craft* of interviewing.

Many can simply be summarized. Some rules and guidelines for interviewing may easily be recognized by novice writers—others, however, are matters of psychology and perception that may require some experience.

Understanding these advanced principles and ideas may help the novice or intermediate interviewer obtain much more valuable interviews. (The techniques and guidelines in this chapter refer largely to the person-to-person interview. On occasion, however, the telephone interview or the mail response may be used.)In this chapter, suggestions and guidelines are offered, generally in order from the basic to the most advanced and in the most logical order.*Read all you can about your subject before the interview*. If you work for a newspaper, ask your newspaper librarian to dig up back files for you. Read every- thing in newspaper or magazine form that has been published about your subject.

This will allow you to...*Prepare in advance*. Write down likely questions. Both DeWitt Reddick and John Brady refer to the Boy Scout motto: *Be prepared*. There is no substitute for preparation. If you prepare for two or three or four avenues of interview development, the more information you will obtain and the less likely you will be to be caught off guard mentally during an interview.*Time the interview to fit your subject's schedule.* Change your own schedule first, if possible. Don't inconvenience the subject's time for your own schedule.

If you have a *deadline* for the story, however, mention that. The subject will usually be willing to meet with you at a time that will allow you to complete the article prior to the deadline.*Be patient.* If you are interviewing someone on the edges of the sports world, this might be the first time they have been interviewed. Many people are unac- quainted with reporters or interviewers. In "The Interview or The Only Wheel in

Town," the *Journalism Monographs'* Eugene J. Webb and Jerry Salancik (1966) suggested that there may be problems regarding your subject's answers:

1. The potential source may not know the information (the reporter seeks).
2. The source may be aware and want to tell but lacks the verbal skills to doso.
3. The source may be willing but not want to tell.
4. The source may be willing but unable to produce the information because it is buried beyond his conscious ability to recall it. (p. 21)

Ask questions in chronological order. If you are interviewing for a personality portrait or profile, proceeding through these five areas may give you comprehensive answers:

1. Birth—location and date—and youth;
2. Education;
3. Military service if any—dates, specialty, and location;
4. Marriage—including spouse's name and age of children, if any;

5. Career—to date.

Ask for dates. Ages, dates of marriage, beginning of career, career achievements— the subject's ages at those times. These dates supply readers with a ready reference to parallel their own life to the life of your subject.

Ask why questions. These demand the subject explain positions, career choices, and beliefs.

Why do you believe such-and-such?

If this is your best season as player, *why*?

Why is this team better than last year?

Why do you believe your coaching techniques are better than your opposition?

In addition to *why* questions, the *how or how did it happen* question may be equally important. Professional athletes may not be articulate enough to explain why something happened—why they have a particularly distinct golf swing or why they have a trademark style, or even why they chose a particular play at a particular time.

It might be more productive to ask: "Show me what you do—demonstrate your swing for me.... Show me what you did at that time.... *How* did you do that?"

In watching the *how's* of their technique, you may also be able to determine the *why's*—why they play the way they do.

Get a telephone number for any additional trivial details you may need to call *back for.* Don't drive across town for two or three additional questions if you can make a telephone call. If the subject has an unlisted telephone, promise you won't disclose it to others, and keep your promise.

Interview all possible sources. If you are interviewing Bonnie Blair or Picabo Street, two U.S. winners in the 1994 Olympics, for instance, ask them who else should be interviewed: parents, coaches, teammates, or others. The question often arises: How do I know when I have enough interviews for a major story? The cynical answer is: When is your deadline? How much time do you have, working backward from that time, to get interviews done and the story written?

The ideal answer is to interview until you come full circle. During every interview, you should ask, "Who else should I talk to?" If you are interviewing A for a major story, and A tells you to talk to B, C, and D, you work your way around the subject until persons X, Y, and Z tell you to see B, C, and D.

When you have run out of interview subjects around A, it's time to start to write the story; or, when you begin to hear the same anecdotes from a variety of subjects, it's time to begin the writing process.It is seldom good practice to arbitrarily limit yourself to five interviews or six or seven.

How do you know that the eighth or ninth or tenth would not have given you the best material for your story?*Don't be a cheerleader.* Asking a question like, "Sure was a good game, wasn't it coach?" leads to a laconic answer: "Yep." That is a very small crumb to use in your story. Even breaking the ice in a conversation with a comment like that is a lame beginning.*Be aware that many coaches and some players expect you to "be on their side."*

Indiana basketball coach Bobby Knight and many others adopt an "us against the media" attitude. As a sports writer, you have at least four choices when encountering these defensive (no pun intended) individuals:

1. Negotiate with them if they show an aggressive attitude toward you as aninterviewer.
2. Interview assistant coaches—or "interview around the subject."
3. Trade notes with a reporter from a noncompeting publication. If you workfor a newspaper that covers Bobby Knight's team, trade notes with a news-paper reporter in a noncompeting area.

4. Use the coach's belligerent attitude in the story—as accurately as possible.If he gets into trouble from the story, that's his problem, not your problemas a reporter.

Don't fail to ask the obvious.

Why did you, coach, go for that field goal instead of a pass? Why did you play for a tie instead of a win?

Why did you call for that particular play on the 37 with a minute and a half left in the game?

Games seldom explain themselves fully. Ask about the key play that won the game—or lost it—for a particular coach or team.

If you are a print reporter, learn as much as you can about tape recorders, *modem connections, video cameras, and the like.* Radio and TV reporters, for the most part, are adept at electronic equipment. Print reporters are less so. But there is little reason why, in these days, print reporters should not use quality tape re- corders. And there are several good reasons why they *should.*

OPENING UP

Sports journalism in many ways remains a paradox. In the hierarchy of professional journalism it has been traditionally viewed disparagingly as the 'toy department', a bastion of easy living, sloppy journalism and 'soft' news. Within the British context sports journalism, until recently, has been largely absent from journalism education and practice and similarly invisible among the growing critical literature from within media and communication studies which examines issues in and around journalism.

However, commercially sports journalism has always mattered to newspapers and the popular press specifically. What has changed in the last decade in the British newspaper market has been the explosion in the volume and range of sports journalism that one now finds across the media. For some, the fact that newspapers such as *The Times* and *The Daily Telegraph* now regularly can devote up to a third of editorial space to coverage of sports is another example of the 'dumbing down of society', with journalism heavily implicated in this process.

This book argues that this expansion in sports journalism actually says something more complex about the evolving relationship between journalism, the media and popular culture, and offers challenges to both critics and educators involved not only in teaching about journalism but in critically evaluating its wider cultural, social and political impact.

Sports journalism has also been implicated in the construction of various sporting discourses that often connect with wider issues of gender, race, ethnicity and national identity formation. Within media and communication studies a body of work concerned with the role of the media, and in part sports journalism, in this process of identity formation is now well established (Whannel, 1992; Blain et al., 1993; O'Donnell, 1994; Garland and Rowe, 1999; Wenner, 1998; Rowe, 1999; Boyle and Haynes, 2000; Brookes, 2002; Crolley and Hand, 2002; Hand and Crolley, 2005).

Much of this work has focused on the various texts produced by forms of sports journalism and broadcasting and these debates about the role of sporting representation and society have been well addressed by such work. As a result, concerns about representation are not the main focus of this book, although reference is made to this issue where appropriate.

This book is also not a practical guide on how to become a sports journalist. Neither is it overly concerned with outlining the specific aspects of the job that inform the day-to-day working practice of those engaged in sports journalism although, of course, reference to these issues is made where directly relevant. These issues are admirably addressed by Andrews (2005) in his book on sports journalism, in which he examines in detail the challenges and skills involved in the craft of sportswriting across the print, broadcast and online media environments.

Rather, this book is about identifying sports journalism's wider place within the broader field of journalism and journalism studies. The book attempts to offer a historically informed snapshot of some of the issues, debates and challenges that are reshaping the boundaries of contemporary sports journalism, specifically, but not exclusively, within the UK media context.

There are three implicit strands that run through the book, and while they may not always be addressed directly in every chapter, they are important factors in shaping the environment within which contemporary sports journalism operates. These forces are reconfiguring both the sports and the media industries from within which sports journalism emerges. Their varying impact on journalism may be disputed, but globalisation, digitization and marketisation are key underlying aspects of any analysis of contemporary journalism.

GLOBALISATION

There is no doubt that sports have become increasingly global in the contemporary mediated age. The fusion of sports and the media, and television in particular, has helped propel and transform major events such as the FIFA World Cup and the Olympic Games. This is also a process in which sports journalism is deeply implicated.

The American political journalist Franklin Foer (2004) argued that the global nature of sport offered the possibility of the construction of some form of global identity. However, the reality that he found on his travels around the world was a global cultural form that acted as a vehicle for the expression of conflict, tension and a range of deeply rooted local identities. This tension between the global aspect of sport as a cultural form and its intrinsic national or local dimension has also been noted by Rowe (2003). These processes are informed by economic, cultural and ethnic factors, and often reinforced by sports journalism.

Sports journalism offers a fascinating case study in how global and local media interact in contemporary societies. Sport can at times appear global and outward-looking, and can also be local in focus and intensely domestic in its concerns.

While this book is primarily centred on the UK experience, it will also be noticeable the extent to which the development of sports journalism in, say, the United States has helped influence British sports writing. Echoing the earlier point about the local and the global, the book will, however, reinforce the extent to which sports journalism is heavily shaped by the particular patterns of social, cultural and political evolution that shape both the sports and the media industries in the UK.

DIGITISATION

Related to globalisation is digitisation. Digitisation has clearly impacted on journalism in various forms. Within the arena of sports journalism, it has seen the emergence of an increasingly sophisticated battle for control of sports and how they are delivered, reported and made sense of for readers, listeners and viewers.

Previous research (Boyle and Haynes, 2004) has examined the ways in which sports clubs and organisations are attempting to use the new media platforms of the Internet, digital TV and mobile telephony to deliver exclusive content and journalism to spectators. In so doing, many are seeking to bypass the traditional journalistic communication structures and speak directly to their audience.

In the digital age, the sports industry increasingly attempts to police its image through the control of its intellectual property (IP) and the growing use of public relations and other aspects of media management.

For sports journalists, the issue of access to players and information has become more difficult as the commercial stakeholders in the game attempt to use the digital landscape to usurp and bypass traditional sports journalism. There seems little doubt that over the next few years the battle lines will continue to be redrawn as sports seek to extract commercial value from all their assets, while media institutions (in particular those not holding specific coverage rights) will argue for the importance of continuing to journalistically report on all aspects of the sports industry.

MARKETISATION

Marketisation has impacted on both the sports and the media industries. The reporting of the political and economic dimension of sports has become more important in recent years as the commercialisation of the industry across the globe has developed. The sports industry now regularly involves major media and financial institutions as well as government intervention.

This process has helped blur the boundaries between traditional notions of sports journalism and journalism about sports-related activity. The increased centrality of the market in the media industries has helped propel the expansion of a celebrity culture, into which sports stars increasingly find themselves drawn. This development has also shaped aspects of sports journalism where there has been an increase in the number of journalists both freelance and staffers reporting and commenting on this aspect of sports.

Sports journalism and writing is now also seen as a key element of the wider branding of most newspapers as they reposition their appeals in attempts to attract new readers. The general dismantling of a more paternal media system in the UK, and its replacement with a more commercially driven demand-led entity, has both benefited and constrained sports journalism. However, without the introduction of increased competition in the UK television market, and the corresponding explosion in the coverage of sport, there is little doubt that the expansion in sports journalism that is so evident in the UK media market would simply not have happened to the same degree.

A combination of the global expansion of sport, the new opportunities offered by digital media and sport's growing commercial value have helped to extend the range of opportunities for those graduates seeking to break into sports journalism. And of course, the expansion of the sports industry and the range of commercial and political stakeholders involved also mean that rigorous, uncomplicit journalism is required in this area as never before. This represents a major ethical challenge for contemporary sports journalism.

The book is also concerned with the professional context within which sports journalism is positioned. Is the often used analogy of the 'toy department' still valid? Are sports journalists simply 'fans with a typewriter' or laptops as it would be these days? Or, as the range of sports journalism has expanded is it more accurate to talk about journalism about sports, in its entire wider context, rather than simply a narrowly defined and niche form of journalism, labelled, sports journalism.

Sports journalism's roots developed long before Sports Illustrated and ESPN. Sports writers, although mocked in early days for not being serious writers, now revel in an industry worth billions. From the Internet, newspapers, radio and television to the movies and magazines, content is vast and packed with heart racing photos and videos of games, plays, moments, and victories and losses.

Athletes jockey for a place in the news and the cameras always seem to be rolling, and now for the history of sports journalism.

1789 IN THE BEGINNING

Horses, which some paleontologists believe may have originally evolved from dinosaurs, may have the right to claim the first glimmers of sports journalism. In 1727, The Racing Calendar offers information about races and their results. In 1791, The General Stud book is added. The site History World, www.historyworld.net explains that the English were curious about the lineage of their horses too.

Boxing is a popular sport in London. Champion Daniel Mendoza writes a book about the sport. It is called The Art of Boxing. Mendoza goes on to lose the title from John Jackson, known as

Gentleman Jack. According to the site, his name "is more for the circle of friends than his fighting style."

From these times, the publications for men told of great battles between men and if they fought for fun, exercise or settling a wager. Even back then, the details involving blood, bruises and broken bones excited men.

The sport gained in popularity after readers caught on to the idea of beating someone without getting in trouble. Women were not allowed in any sports establishment in London, and most had no desire to change this rule.

In the 1800s, the idea of basketball is started and other sports follow. The times of our country demanded attention be placed on work and home, not recreational activities. In the early part of the 1900s, America dealt with the full impact of the Industrial Revolution and World War l. The times preceding the First World War brought a new life to the game of golf, which has its early origins in Scotland. About.com explains the Scots claim they invented the game; however, there is some speculation that they may have evolved it instead.

1900S EARLY DAYS

Golf is a popular game and has several magazines devoted to it. This includes The American Golfer. Published by Conde Nast, it was founded in the early half of the 1900s. Its covers have featured golf greats, including Bobby Jones, Walter Hagen and Byron Nelson.

This information comes from World Golf, www.worldgolf.com.

The Depression and World War ll brought a halt to sports as scores of men and women left home to defend the country. Children and youth continued to play. Yet, it was after the war that sports celebrated a rebirth.

1954 THE BIRTH OF SPORTS ILLUSTRATED

Sports Illustrated is arguably one of the most popular magazines for sports journalism.

Even though its first issue was not released until August of 1954, the executives at Time, Inc realized its potential when World War II ended and sports became a major recreational activity. The first cover features slugger Eddie Matthews of the Milwaukee Braves. In top condition, it could be worth $150-$200, a review site for EBay, www.reviews.ebay.com, reads.

Back then, executives did not know much about sports journalism. The magazine changed from one week to the next as they tried different ideas. Still, the topics offered readers a full range of information and photographs regarding different sports. These included everything from football and basketball to gymnastics and even bullfighting! The earlier issues featured how-to tips too.

Once the readership became established, executives enticed fans with "a three-page center foldout of 1954 Topps baseball cards." Willie Mays, Jackie Robinson and Ted Williams were featured on the cards, which were "printed on the same paper stock as the magazine."

The term, "Sports Illustrated swimsuit issue" dates back to the early 1960s when executives began pondering the idea. In January 1964, the first issue showing a woman with a white two-piece suit caused an instant reaction. The site explains that the picture is "tame by today's standards."

In the early days of the magazine African Americans did not have equality or respect. Through time, and many long fights, this is changing. Sports Illustrated is one place to feature the black athletes. These include two popular personalities, Muhammad Ali and Michael Jordan. The site claims, "They have been featured on the front cover more times than any other athletes."

The front cover of SI, as it is called by many readers and fans, featured non-athlete faces, including Bob Hope, Ernest Hemingway and President John F. Kennedy. These issues, if they can be found and in top condition, have enormous value.

SPORTS JOURNALISM NOW

Today, Sports Illustrated is branching out with an issue for youth. Its content is designed to encourage involvement in sports, provide information about reducing injuries, and highlighting major names like Michael Johnson and others.

The editors know the youth are influenced by what they include in each issue. In response, they often include ads by stars that encourage youth to avoid drugs and alcohol, stay in school and remain clear of trouble. It is one of the few magazines geared towards youth.

Newspapers provided sports journalism from the first days of publishing.

The coverage was basic and sparse. Writers often did not know much about the sports themselves. Occasionally, a sportswriter would actually have a working knowledge of the game.

Times changed when accuracy and details became more important than yellow journalism. This was when the focus was on the sensational bits of news and facts often went unverified, if they were facts at all.

As credible papers debuted, sportswriters needed more knowledge of the sport they covered. Now, many companies and stations want actual experience form their writers. This makes former athletes more valuable and offers them a chance to stay "in the game" instead of disappearing from sight.

The Internet, radio shows and television offer sports journalism. The depth of coverage is intense and high point players garner attention and fame. The stories by sportswriters cover more than scores and highlights; they also cover future plays, fears of coaches, personal snapshots of players, typical road life adventures, issues with recruiting and trades.

It is not just the fans who pay attention to the sportswriters. Coaches from around the country, scouts and even advertisers watch and listen. Nike, Spalding and other big names use the information provided by the sportswriters when looking for the next big idea. They want to see who will be the next star. The whole wants to know too, and sportswriters have plenty of answers.

A GOLDEN AGE; A BEGINNING

Known as the Golden Age of Sports, the decade or so between the end of World War I and the beginning of the great depression was described as a decade of change.

America and the world wanted to put the memory of the Great War behind them and enjoy life. The economy was booming because of the war and the automobile was becoming a more common means of transportation.

This freedom allowed America to fall in love with sports through the exploits of Jack Dempsey, Man O' War, The Four Horseman of Notre Dame, and the biggest name of all, Babe Ruth.

The 1920s is also known as the Age of the Spectator as new and bigger stadiums and gymnasiums were being built and the radio became the favorite medium of news travel. Fans were able to keep up with their favorite teams therefore newspapers increased their coverage of sports.

For the first time, large numbers of Americans began to pay actual money to watch people compete in athletic contest.

During the 1920s, it was baseball that stole the hearts of spectators and became the "national pastime." A right fielder for the New York Yankees was making heads spin by hitting more home runs than any player had ever hit, exciting fans, and becoming the most famous athlete in the United States. Yes, you guessed right, George Herman "Babe" Ruth. Ruth was the perfect hero for the roaring twenties.

It was during this golden age that sportswriters began to emerge. Names like Ring Lardner, Grantlan Rice, Damon Runyon and many more proved to be colorful scribes. The often cynical, witty, romantic, and celebratory prose, however, began to grate on the American people, causing writers to look at heroes as ordinary human beings and at sports in a more critical manner.

Writers during this era were still treated well by the clubs but the writers themselves now had the freedom to report any news, and not just good news. As a direct result, sportswriting became more objective and analytical.

In August of 1954 sports journalism in America was changed forever by the birth of Sports Illustrated magazine. The very first cover issue showed Milwaukee Braves slugger Eddie Matthews taking one of his enviable home run swings.

During its first five years of growth the magazine was aimed at the American middle-class consumer and sports spectator and covered just about any sport it could cover. As years progressed however the magazine began to center on certain sports like baseball, basketball, or football.

The industry began to boom when only 13 years ago, after satisfying himself that there must be absolute limits to human strength, speed, agility and endurance, the U.S. Olympic team track coach, Brutus Hamilton compiled a list of ultimate track and field performances, and records that would never be broken.

However, quite the opposite happened and every year since that list was posted, an athlete has broken the record. There states the facts, that there really are no absolutes in sport, and those athletes have never been as skillful as they are now. This has made the U.S. appetite for sport insatiable and the market tremendous.

Today sport journalist revels in the fact that one out of every five Americans is a steady customer at the local bowling alley; one out of twenty plays golf or tennis. And, when they are not playing the sport, they are most certainly watching, making the need for reporting bigger than it ever has been. As a matter of fact, for sport's biggest bills, television more often than not picks up the tab, and sports of all sorts bring out the best of TV, the imagination of its reporters, and the skills of its engineers.

Sports Writer

A sports writer has the responsibility to both entertain and inform people about what is occurring within the world of sports. Some sports writers focus on one particular sport whereas others write on all sports within a given area. Some sports writers are syndicated or are published in more than one newspaper and others may write for a local newspaper or even for a website, blog, magazine or TV show.

Sports writers may work freelance and sell individual stories to various news outlets or they may work for a given publication. Those sports writers that do freelance work pick their sporting events to cover, whereas those that work for a publication are usually assigned stories. Both types of sports writers have to be able to capture the excitement and interest of the reader as well as provide an accurate depiction of the sporting event or issue that they are writing on.

A sports writer must be willing to work long hours and still make deadlines for printing. Most writers now use computer word processing programs that make editing and revising a bit easier, and also allows for submissions by email to meet tight deadlines. Creativity, a very complete understanding of the sport, good rapport with athletes, coaches and managers as well as an ability to write are all important for a sports writer. An interest in news as well as keeping up-to-date on all issues with regards to the sports community is also important on a daily basis.

Common work activities include:

- Attending games and sporting events to be able to write accurately and effectively on the events of the game.

- Writing insightful, informative and original stories on various aspects of sports from human interest on up to game day results.
- Researching, networking and developing contacts in the sporting world that can provide accurate and up-to-date information on various aspects of the sport.
- Meeting with publishers, editors and writing teams to develop and obtain assignments or ideas for possible stories.
- Keeping in constant contact with athletes, owners, coaches and managers and using high ethical standards to avoid compromising the writing.

3

Children and Sports Media

INTRODUCTION

The Amateur Athletic Foundation of Los Angeles has had a longstanding interest in the role of sport media. The foundation's interest in the topic derives from a belief that the sport media reflect and help shape public attitudes about sport and the people who participate in sport.

Furthermore, studying the sport media can provide insights into broader social attitudes about a range of people and issues.

The AAF sponsored a national conference, in 1989, called Getting Over the Hurdle: Race and Gender in Sports Media. Following the conference, the foundation funded its first media study *Gender Stereotyping in Televised Sport*, published in 1990.

That report was followed by *Coverage of Women's Sport in Four Daily Newspapers* (1991) and *Gender Stereotyping in Televised Sport: A Follow-up to the 1989 Study* (1994). A third edition of the television study will be released in 2000.

The primary focus of the foundation's activity is youth sport. While the ways in which television and newspapers cover women's sport clearly have an impact on children's perceptions of gender roles and sport, this is the first AAF media study to deal exclusively with young people.

In April 1999, the AAF commissioned Statistical Research, Inc. of Westfield, N.J. to conduct a national survey among children ages 8 to 17 to explore their exposure to sports through various forms of media.

The primary purpose of the study was to measure how many youngsters use sport media, what kind of media they use, how often they use the media, what sports and what media "products" were most popular among young consumers, and in what social contexts did media use occur. Although *Children and Sport Media* does not evaluate the impact of sport media on young people, it is the foundation's hope that this report will provide a starting point for researchers who wish to examine how, if at all, the sport media contribute to the development of children's perceptions and values.

The study looks at eight major forms of media:

- Television
- Radio
- Newspapers
- Books
- Magazines
- Video games
- The Internet
- Movies

Survey questions sought to determine exposure to sports via each medium. Follow-up questions established a context of use for each medium. In addition, interviewers asked questions to determine personal and household demographics.

This report provides important findings and points out those instances where responses vary among major subgroups. It does not attempt to examine all responses to all questions for all subsets of the population. That level of detail can be found in the tabulation volumes provided separately to the AAF.

This report is organized by topic. Therefore, the sequence in which the subjects appear in the report is not necessarily the exact sequence in which the questions were asked in the interview.

The data have been weighted and sample balanced. Weighting was based on the number of eligible children ages 8 to 17 in the household. Data were sample balanced to U.S. Census estimates of the age and gender distributions of the children, and to the race and Hispanic origin distributions of the households.

Interviews for this study took place between April 12 and May 16, 1999. SRI completed a total of 480 interviews. The response rate was 47 percent.

CRICKET IN INDIA: OBSTACLE FOR OTHER SPORTS?

Cricket has become the most powerful force in sports as well as entertainment domain in India. Although cricket does not enjoy the official status of being the national sport in India, it commands much more excitement and a greater fan following than the other sports including the national sport, Hockey. You can't find a single sport in India which could boast of being even in contest with cricket when it comes to popularity and revenue generation.

The current nexus of Bollywood with cricketing fraternity in itself speaks for the huge following this game enjoys in the country. The great interest for the game on the part of bigwigs of Bollywood like Sahrukh and Preity Zinta, to name a few, shouldn't be merely discerned as their love for the game. There is a lot that follows this symbiotic relation between the two-name, fame, and above all monetary benefits. But every now and then people come out with scathing comments against cricket being the culprit of engulping other sports in India. But, is it true?

Some time back, Youth Affairs and Sports Minister of India, Mr. M.S. Gill, who seemed quite perturbed by the stature of cricket in the country in contrast to other sports had said-"Television, commercialization and the advertising world have promoted cricket to an extent that it has become a Mount Everest which is badly affecting other sports in the country." The sports minister and other critics, in their own rights, may be genuine in claiming the fact that there is no space left by cricket and forerunners of the game for other sports, but one can't deny the fact that where cricket stands today is a result of foresightedness and perseverance.

All these dominance and money pouring in hasn't come to the game in a fortnight. In fact, other games could take a leaf out of cricket's chapter for enhancing their power and existence among the sporting fraternity and masses.

Who would like to invest in such a venture where there seems to be no profit? After all, this is a game of profitable association where both investor as well as the game get benefited; and on the first look, cricket stands way above head and shoulders when pitted against other sports. The cricket mania in India would leave an onlooker amazed and wonderstruck and no doubt it rules the roost. You could easily find the takers of the game from the scanty streets of a suburb to high locales of a city through the remote villages and countryside.

India has never been a great sporting nation. In its heydays, hockey was looked upon by the nation when we were world beaters and enjoyed world dominance; but no sooner did it tread the path of failures, it went into oblivion and the lackluster performances through the decades was quite ominous. As a substitute, cricket was there to grab the opportunity and has been the solitary reaper as far as reaping rich dividends is concerned.

You can't take away the credit which the cricket as a game has earned in the last two to three decades. Pre world cup triumph in 1983, it was just like any other ordinary sport in the country and even behind hockey. That world cup triumph brought about frenzy in the sport lovers of the country who apart from hockey yearned of being world beaters. That triumph is so dearly cherished to these days. Since then, the cricketing juggernaut has every so often provided something to cheer about with the performance and excitement it has in store. India often finds place among the top teams of cricket, and has certain world beaters in its ranks like Sachin Tendulkar, Rahul Dravid, Anil Kumble, Kapil Dev, Sunil Gavaskar, Virender Sehwag and so on.

Today, cricket is a religion in the country and a player like Sachin is god. Instead of accusing cricket as an obstacle in the progress of other sports, it should be perceived as an epitome of intellectual foresightedness which has enthralled masses with a rich blend of performance and excitement. Today, we boast of being the boss of the game in the world. We kind of run the world cricket with the revenue generated through the game in India and also we have a say in any administrative policies.

See the antagonism in authority enjoyed by the cricket board and hockey federation of the country. Hockey is run by superpowers of the game comprising of Germany, Australia and Holland and we Indians are mere puppets in their hands. All the rules and regulations are of their liking and cater to their taste while we go down to them in every aspect of the game. Had we been performing, the scenario would have been altogether different. Our classical approach has been ruined by their power game.

Atleast in cricket, this is not the case. The post Sydney saga, where we forced ICC to sack the umpires in question, sprouts our stature in world cricket, which wouldn't have been possible had we not been a dominant force to reckon. We can also boast of having two cricket leagues which attract cricketers from all quarters, so what is there to complain? These are the heydays for cricket in India- just sit back and enjoy!

Sports journalism is a form of journalism that reports on sports topics and events. While the sports department within some newspapers has been mockingly called the *toy department*, because sports journalists do not concern themselves with the 'serious' topics covered by the news desk, sports coverage has grown in importance as sport has grown in wealth, power and influence.

Sports journalism is an essential element of any news media organization. Sports journalism includes organizations devoted entirely to sports reporting–newspapers such as *L'Equipe* in France, *La Gazzetta dello Sport* in Italy, and the now defunct *Sporting Life* in Britain, American magazines such as *Sports Illustrated* and the *Sporting News*, all-sports talk radio stations, and television networks like ESPN.

HISTORY OF SPORTS JOURNALISM

Since the start of competition, writers have covered sports in one way or another. Sports journalism has been traced all the way back to the time of 850 B.C.E. when the great Greek Homer wrote about the first known draw in Wrestling, as Achilles raised the hands of both Ajax and Odysseus in victory. The sports of wrestling, throwing, boxing, and racing were all wrote on in early Greece.

While sports writing has existed for some time, it did not come prevalent until recently. In the middle 1800s American writers began to write exclusively as sports writers, but they were still few in number. During the time before the 1900s sports writing existed, but was still not widely accepted. It was not until 1914 that sports was written and spread in circulation, and the job of a sports editor was considered an actual job.

The Pioneering Period 1785-1835

Sports journalism during this time was obscure because of the Revolutionary War from 1775 to 1783. In 1790, Benjamin Franklin had several quotes in news publications about swimming, and the The New York Magazine had several articles written on sports.

In the early 1800s, the New York Post, Charleston Courier, and Richmond Enquirer were just some of the publications that were including sports in their papers.

While Boxing was still not accepted as a sport because of its danger, in 1823 a full length story was put into the New York Evening Post, and was marked as the first time this much emphasis was put on its inclusion. English publications such as the Sportsman's Repository and Pierce Egan's Boxiana were in circulation as well.

Growing Acceptance

This period was very important in the growth of sports journalism, as the "penny papers" were looking for new, exciting stories to appeal to their readers. Sports began to grow at a quicker pace after 1850 because of the introduction of baseball, and new interest in team sports in general. With the higher interest in sports, came more stories about the topic and several publications like the New York Herald and the Spirit of the Times recorded sports events in their papers.

During the Golden Age, the importance of news increased and thus, the amount of sports covered increased as well. It was during this time that the average amount of sports coverage had its largest increase from the decade before with 10.4 columns being dedicated to it and 14.6 percent of advertising space. "It appears that when the papers doubled in number of pages, they doubled the size of the sports section. This was only reasonable, since reader-interest surveys rated certain features of the sports section higher than anything else except the most striking news story, the comics, and picture pages" (Heath 1951).

It was not until the 1870's that separate departments were set up for sports in newspapers. The first came when Joseph Pulitzer bought the New York World; he was also the first to hire a sports editor–in 1883.

Many of the major cities copied Pulitzer over the next few years, and by 1892 every large newspaper had a sports editor. However, during this time sports news was condensed into two or three columns of coverage, but it would soon change.

The birth of basketball in 1891, and the introduction of the American Bowling Congress in 1895 helped build the base of sports coverage. 1890 is often considered as the turning point for sports journalism as many sports were introduced. Baseball became the "national pastime" and its stars began to impact the news world. Babe Ruth and the New York Yankees had tremendous sports coverage during the 1923 World Series and is considered one of the best covered sports events of the time.

Continued Expansion

The 1930's marked the first time newspapers hired executive sports editors to oversee all content produced by the newspaper. As the 1940s came along, sports cartoons became a big part of the sports page with Willard Mullin of the New York World-Telegram and Al Papas of The Sporting News leading the industry.

The creation of the Associated Press sports wire on April 16, 1945 helped put sports into the national scope. It was also around this time that sports became worthy of being front page news.

Perhaps the biggest effect on sports journalism occurred when the television was introduced in the 1950s. Baseball and Football saw a large increase in sports coverage in the television industry, and sportswriters were forced to adapt. Newspapers became the second hand method for receiving sports news, because television offered all the news of a newspaper with pictures.

Sports Journalists' Access

Sports teams are not always very accommodating to journalists. In the United States, teams tend to be more accommodating. They allow reporters into locker rooms for interviews and some extra information, and provide extensive information support, even if reporting it is unfavorable to them.

Elsewhere in the world, particularly in the coverage of soccer, the journalist's role is often barely tolerated by the clubs and players.

Sports journalists, like any other reporters, must do their own reporting to find the story rather than simply relying on information given to them by the sports team, institution or coaching staff. Sports journalists must verify facts given to them by the teams and organizations they are covering. Often, coaches, players or sports organization management rescind sports journalists' access credentials in retaliation for printing accurate yet disparaging information about a team, player, coach or coaches, or organization.

Access for sports journalists is usually easier for professional and intercollegiate sports such as American football, ice hockey, basketball, baseball, and football.

Famous Pioneers

Grantland Rice

Grantland Rice was a early innovator for sports journalism and is best known for his work covering college football teams starting in 1925. Rice is also the writer known for naming the Notre Dame backfield of 1924 after the "Four Housemen of the Apocalypse." He covered exceptional athletes like Babe Ruth, Knute Rockne, and Bobby Jones, among others, helping make them into American icons. Rice has a scholarship given in his name by Vanderbilt University for a freshman intending to become a professional sports writer.

Henry Chadwick

Henry Chadwick was known as the father of baseball for his work editing The Beadle Baseball Player, the first guide for sale on baseball. He was one of the first promoters of sports journalism and helped start the National Baseball Club.

Leonard Koppett

Kopett was an established and influential sports writer who wrote for The Sporting News, New York Times, and New York Post among others. His best work was in baseball, writing stories on the game, and the inspirations that come from it. He received the Curt

Gowdy media award by the Basketball Hall of Fame in 1994 and the J.G Taylor Spink Award by the Baseball Hall of Fame in 1992.

Socio-political Significance

Major League Baseball once gave print journalists a special role in its games; they were named official scorers and kept statistics that were considered part of the official record of the league. Active sportswriters were removed from this role in 1980. Although their statistical judgment calls could not affect the outcome of a game, there was still the perception of a conflict of interest.

Sports stories often transcend the games themselves and take on socio-political significance; Jackie Robinson breaking the color barrier in baseball is a good example. Modern controversies regarding the compensation of top athletes, the use of anabolic steroids and other, banned performance-enhancing drugs, and the cost to local and national governments to build sports venues and related infrastructure, especially for the Olympic Games, show that sports still can intrude onto the news pages.

Sportswriters face much more deadline pressure than most other reporters, because sporting events tend to occur late in the day and closer to the deadlines many organizations must observe. Yet, they are expected to use the same tools as news journalists, and to uphold the same professional and ethical standards. They must take care not to show bias for any team. Sports journalists usually must also gather and use voluminous performance statistics for teams and individual athletes in most sports.

Many of the most talented and respected print journalists have been sportswriters.

Sports Journalism in Europe

The tradition of sports reporting attracting some of the finest writers in journalism can be traced to the coverage of sport in Victorian England, where several modern sports—such as association football, cricket, athletics and rugby—were first organized and codified into something resembling what we would recognize today.

Cricket, somewhat like baseball in the United States, has regularly attracted the most elegant of writers due to its esteemed place in society. The *Manchester Guardian*, in the first half of the twentieth century, employed Neville Cardus as its cricket correspondent as well as its music critic. Cardus was later knighted for his services to journalism. One of his successors, John Arlott, who became a worldwide favorite because of his radio commentaries on the BBC, and was also known for his poetry.

The first London Olympic Games in 1908 attracted such widespread public interest that many newspapers assigned their very best-known writers to the event. The *Daily Mail* even had Sir Arthur Conan Doyle at the White City Stadium to cover the finish of the first ever 26-mile, 385-yard Marathon.

Such was the drama of that race, in which Dorando Pietri collapsed within sight of the finishing line when leading, that Conan Doyle led a public subscription campaign to see the gallant Italian, having been denied the gold medal through his disqualification, awarded a special silver cup, which was presented by Queen Alexandra.

And the public imagination was so well caught by the event that annual races in Boston, Massachusetts, and London, and at future Olympics, were henceforward staged over exactly the same, 26-mile, 385-yard distance, the official length of the event worldwide to this day.

The London race, called the Polytechnic Marathon and originally staged over the 1908 Olympic route from outside the royal residence at Windsor Castle to White City, was first sponsored by the *Sporting Life*, which in those Edwardian times was a daily newspaper which sought to cover all sporting events, rather than just a betting paper for [horse racing]] and greyhounds that it became in the years after the Second World War.

In France, *L'Auto*, the predecessor of *L'Equipe*, had already played an equally influential part in the sporting fabric of society when it announced in 1903 that it would stage an annual bicycle race around the country. The Tour de France was born, and sports journalism's role in its foundation is still reflected today in the leading rider wearing a yellow jersey–the color of the paper on which *L'Auto* was published (in Italy, the Giro d'Italia established a similar tradition, with the leading rider wearing a jersey the same pink color as the sponsoring newspaper, *La Gazetta*).

Specialist Sports Agencies

The 1950s and 1960s saw a rapid growth in sports coverage, both in print and on broadcast media. It also saw the development of specialist sports news and photographic agencies. For example, photographer Tony Duffy founded the picture agency AllSport in south London shortly after the 1964 Tokyo Olympics, and, through some outstanding photography (such as Duffy's iconic image of the American long jumper Bob Beamon flying through the air towards his world record at the 1968 Mexico City Olympics) and the astute marketing of its images, saw the business grow into a multi-million pound, worldwide concern that ultimately would be bought and renamed Getty Images.

McIlvanney and Wooldridge, who died in March 2007[1] aged 75, both enjoyed careers that saw them frequently work in television. During his career, Wooldridge became so famous that, like the sports stars he reported upon, he hired the services of IMG, the agency founded by the American businessman, Mark McCormack, to manage his affairs. And Glanville wrote several books, including novels, as well as scripting the memorable official film to the 1966 World Cup staged in England.

Investigative Journalism and Sport

Since the 1990s, the growing importance of sport, its impact as a global business and the huge amounts of money involved from sponsorship and in the staging of the Olympic Games and football World Cups, has also attracted the attention of well-known investigative journalists. The sensitive nature of the relationships between sports journalists and the subjects of their reporting, as well as declining budgets experienced by most Fleet Street newspapers, has meant that such long-term projects have often emanated from television documentary makers.

Tom Bower, with his 2003 sports book of the year *Broken Dreams*, which analyzed British football (soccer), followed in the tradition established a decade earlier by Andrew Jennings and Vyv Simson with their controversial investigation of corruption within the International Olympic Committee. Jennings and Simson's *The Lords of the Rings* in many ways predicted the scandals that were to emerge around the staging of the 2002 Winter Olympics in Salt Lake City; Jennings would follow-up with two further books on the Olympics and one on FIFA, the world football body. Likewise, award-winning writers Duncan Mackay, of *The Guardian*, and Steven Downes unraveled many scandals involving doping, fixed races and bribery in international athletics in their 1996 book, *Running Scared*, which offered an account of the threats by a senior track official that led to the suicide of their sports journalist colleague, Cliff Temple.

But the writing of such exposes—referred to as "spitting in the soup" by Paul Kimmage, the former Tour de France professional cyclist, who now writes for the *Sunday Times*—often requires the view of an outsider who is not compromised by the need of day-to-day dealings with sportsmen and officials, as required by "beat" correspondents.

The stakes can be high when upsetting sport's powers: when in 2007, the English FA opted to switch its multi-million pound contract for UK coverage rights of the FA Cup and England international matches from the BBC to rival broadcasters ITV, one of the reasons cited was that the BBC had been too critical of the performances of the England football team.

SOME LEADERS IN SPORTS JOURNALISM

ESPN

ESPN or the Entertainment and Sports Programming Network launched in 1979 as a sports channel that covered low-awareness sports. Its signature show, Sportscenter, originated to show a larger package of sports highlights than local news programming. Since its inception, ESPN has grown into one of the largest players in the sports media industry.

They currently offer sports television channels of ESPN, ESPN2, ESPNews, ESPNClassic, ESPNU, ESPN Deportes, ESPN International, ESPN Brazil, and ESPN360.com. ESPN also covers sports with their magazine, ESPN sports radio, and their streaming website, ESPN.com.

ESPN fills their sports television stations with coverage and live broadcasting of sporting events from the NBA, NFL, MLB, college football, college basketball, PGA, PTA, PBA, Nascar, WNBA, and others.

Sports Illustrated

Sports Illustrated is a well-known weekly sports magazine that has been covering sports since its inception on August 16, 1954. What started out as a magazine that covered yachting and polo has grown into a news source for all kinds of sports.

The early times of Sports Illustrated were anchored by the outstanding sports journalist of Dan Jenkins, Tex Maule, and Robert Creamer. More recently the great work of writers such as Rick Reilly have helped keep Sports Illustrated as a popular source for sports news.

Fox Sports

Fox broadcasting company entered the world of sports journalism in 1993 when in bid 1.58 billion dollars to be the NFC conference television carrier in 1993 for the NFL. Since then, Fox Sports has become a large part of the sports journalism world with its regional television networks for many parts of the United States, and with its Fox Sports World channel.

Fox Sports carries the rights to the Bowl Championship Series for college football, and also broadcasts NBA, NFL, Nascar, and other major sports leagues.

GLOBALISATION AGGRAVATES PROBLEMS OF SLACK SPORTS JOURNALISM

Let's begin with a familiar, if somewhat increasingly old fashioned, notion that journalism is unique to a culture. That independent, reliable and comprehensive information is something every citizen requires to be free. And that when we are asked to provide something more than this, we subvert democracy.

This idea of a free press has been with us since the first days of democracy and it has survived more or less intact over the years. But in a world of globalisation, which offers through new technologies unprecedented opportunities for communication between communities, we see this fundamental concept under greater pressure than ever.

The balance of power between the powerful elites in society: trade bureaucrats, corporate leaders and political leadership and journalism has never been perfect, but it is more uneven and dangerously out of line than ever before.

I share the frustration of the organisers of Play the Game when the leaders of bodies such as UEFA, FIFA and the IOC are arrogantly dismissive of attempts to engage them in dialogue over the crises within sport.

Theirs is a scandalous neglect of public duty to engage in dialogue and failure to take collective responsibility for what many see as corruption in sport and the poisoning of the ideals and aspirations upon which sport is based.

THE COMPLICITY OF THE MEDIA IN BAD SPORTS JOURNALISM

But the problem is not just that the powerful leaders of world sport are increasingly invisible and unaccountable; media, too, are complicit in this lack of transparency.

The degree of economic interdependence between media and the world of sports whether through advertising, sponsorship or negotiation of television rights has led to complacency and worse in the editorial approach to sports reporting.

Self-censorship is rife, not only because invisible powers work their magic in the news room, but also because journalists themselves often opt for the comforts of close association with their official sources rather than establishing professional distance.

Within sports journalism there is a range of clubs and associations of journalists and writers attached to specific disciplines that have a sometimes unhealthy relationship with sports federations. Who will ask the difficult and awkward questions if the consequences are potentially damaging to the advertising department, to the sponsorship of events or television revenues or may undermine access to covering major sports events?

The problem is that globalisation brings with it a new set of self-centred values. There is less investment in investigative journalism, weaker dialogue and much less risk-taking. Traditional notions of reporting integrated into the larger world of communications with journalism being subsumed into advertising, entertainment, electronic commerce and, increasingly propaganda, in step with the militaristic and unilateralist tone of contemporary world politics.

The growth of media monopolies on a national and global scale have cut deep into the culture of press freedom and diversity upon which notions of democratic pluralism are based.

Media conglomerates have come a long way since William Randolph Hearst used his chain of US newspapers to instigate war with Spain in 1898. But the political punch of concentrated media remains as powerful today as it was 100 years ago.

In Canada, one of these regional groups, CanWest Global has compromised the spirit of journalistic mission and public trust by seeking to impose a centralized editorial policy which from Quebec to the Rocky Mountains provides a corporate media megaphone that uses a network of newspapers and television stations giving access to more than 90 per cent of English-speaking Canada.

In Italy, Mediaset owned by Silvio Berlusconi, the prime minister and media magnate, has a stranglehold on 90 per cent of the country's broadcast media including the public broadcaster. His conflicts of interest are notorious: he is also the owner of Milan football club.

Not to act now would be irresponsible. As George Orwell wrote in his unpublished introduction to Animal Farm, censorship in free societies is infinitely more sophisticated and thorough than in dictatorships because 'unpopular ideas can be silenced, and inconvenient facts kept dark, without any need for an official ban'. Journalists can go along with that or they can demand a change of approach.

Above all, we need to build coalitions, not only within journalism, but also with those in society who are striving for a broader social and moral obligation for journalism. Certainly, we should get back to some basics as we were urged earlier in this conference and perhaps we should take up the challenge of one of the most successful globalisers of all.

In his address to world journalists in the jubilee year 18 months ago Pope John Paul II said: "with its vast and direct influence on public opinion, journalism cannot be guided only by economic forces, profit and special interests. It must instead be felt as a mission carried out in the knowledge that the powerful means of communication have been entrusted to you for the good of all."

MEDIA SPORT CULTURE AN EDUCATION IN THE POLITICS OF ACQUISITION

Sport and exercise professionals generally have a deep, even romantic attachment to sport, and a commitment to the celebration of the body as an object of approved performance. Sport, exercise and physical education have been justified on many grounds, including the promotion of lifelong health and longevity; the distraction and diversion of youth, especially boys, from 'unhealthy' and 'immoral' pursuits; developing self esteem among citizens, including positive attitudes to body image and athletic capability among girls and women; enhancing the combat readiness of the population; encouraging international exchange and understanding; reinforcing and raising levels of sociability, and instilling national pride (Cashmore, 2005; Guttmann, 2004; Horne *et. al.*, 1999).

In all these and other instances, professionals are expected to produce performative benefits through systematic intervention, while at the same time contributing to the development of a sports industry that has continuously modernised, as amateurism gave way to professionalism, and voluntary organizations became components of the burgeoning services sector. Sport and exercise professionals have been progressively integrated with, and implicated in the operations of, the sport industry itself, as the commercial corporate sector has exerted greater power over governments and peak sport organizations.

While the field of sport, exercise and physical education has much to commend it, for every positive dimension there is a negative possibility. For example, much physical activity is far from healthy, causing injury to the body, and, especially in elite sport, creating pressures to play with injuries and to take pain-killing and performance-enhancing drugs with serious health consequences.

Sport, especially among boys from disadvantaged backgrounds, may displace study as an avenue for social mobility, despite the poor statistical chances of 'making it'. Failure at sport may be psychologically damaging, and its competitive culture can encourage cruel and unkind comments about opponents that are deeply wounding. Sport may display and encourage some of the worst displays and practices of sexism and ethnocentrism, while aggressive patriotism and national, racial and ethnic stereotyping are often evident in international competitions (Bairner, 2001; Baker and Boyd, 1997; Birrell and McDonald, 2000; Carrington and McDonald, 2001).

It is important, therefore, that professionals in this division of the 'body industry' have a complete and unvarnished grasp of it. In this paper, I want to trace the outlines of the sport industry and to highlight some of the key facets that shape this important socio-cultural phenomenon. In particular, I will contextualise the structure and practice of contemporary sport, seeking to propose areas of effective intervention for sport and exercise professionals that benefit the institution of sport and its primary constituencies, rather than interests seeking to use sport for their own purposes.

The Media Sports Cultural Complex

In various earlier publications I have used the concept of the media sports cultural complex to highlight the contemporary sport formation (Rowe, 2004a).

In short, I argue that over the last century there has effectively been a merger of two formerly separate institutions – media and sport. This convergence has occurred because each has been able, synergistically, to supply the other with important benefits. For sport to become professional in character and national, international and then global in reach, it could no longer rely on physical spectator presence in stadia that was its economic staple until the mid 20th century.

For the media, especially in electronic form, technological capability for disseminating content had by the same period (the mid 20th century) far exceeded the imagined provision of screen material

(Williams, 1974). Sport helped to fill this emergent televisual space by providing the broadcast media with passionate followers (and so enthusiastic advertisers and sponsors), 'live' action, constant and cyclical news, replays, studio discussion material, and so on.

Sport, at first reluctantly and then enthusiastically, traded media access to events and audiences for broadcast rights revenue, in the process creating the foundation of a celebrity sport star system, and advancing the development of commodity logic within sport (see various contributions to Wenner, 1998).

In many countries (especially in Europe), broadcast sport was developed by national media organizations that saw in the institution of sport a useful means of developing a sense of shared national culture.

It later emerged – as had already been discovered in countries like the United States with mainly privatised broadcast systems – that the televisual sport spectator market could create an exchange value far beyond that of the place-based sport economy (Bernstein and Blain, 2003; see various contributions to Rowe, 2004b).

The separation between amateur and professional sport also advanced the detachment of sportspeople (mainly male) from the neighbourhoods and non-sport occupations in which they were previously embedded, making possible the highly professionalised, lavishly remunerated elite sport typified at its most global level by association football (Whannel, 2001).

These developments, though, could never be confined to the simple idea of more people watching the same modes of sport from a distance performed by better paid athletes.

Sport became pervasive across the entire spectrum of contemporary culture, from the Internet to the cinema, the back page of the newspaper to the gossip columns, prime time television to radio magazine programs, and all the other media spaces where it could be shaped and shape itself to diverse audiences (Boyle and Haynes, 2000; Rowe, 2004a).

As sport moved from neighbourhoods and stadia to highly dispersed, technologically mediated sites of reception, it articulated with many other domains of culture and commerce. Sport came to be used to attract audiences to the screen, audio, print and now online and mobile telephonic sites where advertised goods and services and corporate brands could be exposed, and, indeed, sold as a consumer item in its own right.

The social institution of sport can be seen, therefore, to have been both transformed by major cultural, economic and technological changes accelerating across the societal spectrum in late- and post-modernity, but also to have been a key vehicle for the furtherance and, indeed, the contestation of those same changes.

I and colleagues have previously described elsewhere the five simultaneous, uneven, interconnected processes which characterize the present moment in sport: Globalization, Governmentalization, Americanization, Televisualization, and Commodification (GGATaC). They are in turn governed by a New International Division of Cultural Labour (NICL). (Miller *et. al.*, 2001: 4).

By this we mean that sport is both a pivotal change agent and testing ground for these major transformative processes that do not constitute a coherent set of developments, but, instead, can be regarded as influencing, by turns systematically and chaotically, the fabric of contemporary socio-cultural existence.

In summary, the NICL has opened up new flows of professional sporting labour around the world, especially when sourced inexpensively from less to the benefit of more affluent nations. Globalization (Maguire, 1999) is encouraging greater portability of people, ideas, capital, technologies and media messages around the world, but at the same time is provoking substantial anti-globalization sentiment, just as dedicated, Americanized cultural exports may be embraced, resented or fail to 'take' in foreign soils (as with the failure of American football to establish itself in other countries despite expensive marketing campaigns).

The traditional sport doctrine of fair play and respect for opponents that encourages a self-controlled citizenry may be contradicted by xenophobic populist campaigns trading on unpleasant national stereotypes (on both sides). Free-to-air television coverage of major sports events may give way on commercial grounds to subscription television, leading to protests at the restriction of its reach and calls for government regulation. Traditional sport clubs may become, or take on the appearance of, franchises, provoking objections from fans that "our team is not for sale".

In other words, the world of sport is perpetually one of contestation and uncertainty, its balance of forces disturbed by its combination of appeal to collective popular sentiment and political economic calculation.

The media are deeply implicated in all these processes and disputes because they have the capacity to uncouple (at least partially) sport from place and so to create global sport spectacles, while also offering the multifarious ways of 'reading' them from different vantage points (see, for example, the special issue of *Inter-Asia Cultural Studies*, 2004 addressing the 2002 Korea-Japan World Cup; Roche, 2000; Tomlinson and Young, 2006).

The recent World Cup of Association Football in Germany, for example, garnered huge television audiences, with the British Broadcasting Corporation (BBC) reporting that:

- Global television audiences for the start of the World Cup were up 26% compared with the 2002 tournament, according to a report.
- The most popular game of the first five days was Brazil's victory over Croatia, seen by an average 60 million people.
- The research was carried out by media analysts Initiative in 23 countries.
- They say more people are watching this time because matches are shown at more convenient times than the 2002 World Cup in Japan and South Korea. (BBC, 2006: n.p.)

There is a considerable interest in the size of TV sports audiences for global mega-media sports events because they confer legitimacy on events themselves, offering a seemingly unequivocal measure of global interest at cultural level.

These statistics can be used to attract capital in its orthodox form, but can also be converted into geo-political currency. For example, the Seoul 1988 Summer Olympics were used explicitly to signal the unrecognised, elevated position of that country as an economic power and political force (Larson and Park, 1993), the 1995 Rugby World Cup and the forthcoming 2010 World Cup of Association Football presented as clear markers of national progress of the post-apartheid Republic of South Africa, and the forthcoming 2008 Beijing Summer Olympics realising and symbolising China's integration with world polity, sport and business.

These national symbols of social and political progress are connected to the economic sphere through the notion that the country is 'open for business' and able to manage with efficiency and panache a major sport spectacle (Toohey, and Veal, 2000) which is an ironic twist of the 1960s civil rights chant, 'the whole world is watching'. Some of the world may be watching directly through sport tourism (Hinch and Higham, 2004; Weed and Bull, 2004) and, in greater numbers by reading the observational reporting of print journalists, but above all it is watching through television.

The commercial value of this TV sport audience is of such consequence that the Fédération Internationale de Football Association (FIFA) commissions research and publicly comments on it in statements, like the one below, that contest claims of time zone viewer sensitivity or falling viewer numbers:

Television coverage at the 2002 FIFA World Cup Korea/Japan™ reached 213 countries, virtually every country in the world, with over 41,100 hours of dedicated programming. This represents a 38% increase in coverage over the 1998 event and set a new record for a single sporting event. Contrary to some expectations, live audiences were not affected by the time zone differences for viewers in Europe and Central and South America. In fact, the cumulative live audience showed an overall increase on the 1998 figures.

Although the overall global audience was down on France 98, this decline was entirely due to the introduction of audited audience measurement in China for the first time, which allows for more accurate reporting ... FIFA has taken the lead in deciding that a more accurate solution needed to be introduced and that this was the right time to do it. As part of this drive towards a more rigorous approach, the viewing figures for 2002 included more audited viewing data than for any previous FIFA World Cup™.

The cumulative audience over the 25 match days of the 2002 event reached a total of 28.8 billion viewers. The corresponding audience for France 98, with unaudited viewing figures for China, reported 33.4 billion. However, if China was excluded from the statistics for both events, the totals show an increase of 431.7 million viewers (+ 2%) for the 2002 FIFA World Cup™.

These impressive figures make the 2002 FIFA World Cup Korea/ Japan™ the most extensively covered and viewed event in television history. (FIFA, 2006: n.p.)

The size of the television audience for global sports events has, as FIFA recognises above, been so routinely exaggerated through careless extrapolation and hyperbole that it has been subject to greater calculative rigour to restore its credibility. This is occurring at a time when the proliferation of media technologies, platforms and viewing sites is making it harder to establish.

Nonetheless, claims of a truly 'global' audience are still illegitimate given the continuing access to television difficulties for many peoples in Africa, Asia and South America.

The problems of even basic TV reception for still sizeable numbers of people is well depicted in a recent Spanish film comedy, *The Great Match (La Gran Final)* (2005), which tells the story of three groups of people living in Mongolia, Niger and the Amazon trying to watch the television broadcast of the 2002 Korea-Japan World Cup final between Brazil and Germany held in Yokohama, Japan.

Theirs is a major battle with aged technology, poor reception and inadequate power to watch a game that, for most in the affluent West, could be watched in the comfort of the living room. That they manage to do so in large, spontaneously formed groups reveals both the very different contexts in which television is viewed, and the difficulties of audience measurement that preoccupy peak sports organizations like FIFA and the International Olympic Committee (IOC).

This emphasis on television audiences and market shares is, of course, closely connected to the economic foundation of the whole event, with its heavy dependency on broadcast rights revenue, advertising and the 'exclusive' partnership/sponsorship of global corporate brands like Coca Cola, Gillette, McDonald's, Hyundai, Yahoo!, Mastercard, Toshiba and adidas.

The last company mentioned, like its competitor Nike, demonstrates how an ancillary market in sportswear and equipment (again, heavily branded) has been created that, ultimately, has turned highly utilitarian clothing and footwear into everyday and even high fashion. This market, in turn, encouraged a fully-formed sport star system, complete with gossip columns and paparazzi photography, to enable the brands to be displayed beyond the field of play, and paid endorsements.

Again, it is impossible to conceive of these key features of contemporary sport without the sustained involvement of the media, of which sport professionals now require an 'insider's' knowledge. A key element of this command of media sport is the perhaps unpalatable appreciation that many sports are so dependent on the media that the latter are shaping it, and that the media have the power to make or break particular sports. It is important, then, to assess the media-sport power balance, and this might be done by examining critically the extent to which the media concentrate on some sports and neglect others, and also lavish attention on some sportspeople and show little interest in others.

Media Sport Hierachies

Both professional and amateur philosophers enjoy engaging with the classic epistemological question, 'If a tree falls in the forest and no one is there, does it still make a sound?' This is a matter that concerns not just whether an event has occurred, but whether it has been observed and so registered and recorded.

In relation to the media and sport, the equivalent might be, ' If a professional sport event is not covered by the professional media, did it happen?'

Of course, for those present it was a real event, and various forms of amateur and semi-professional media, especially those that are internet based, can provide evidence and even a moving (in both senses of the word) record of what occurred. But the extent to which only partially professionalised, 'viral' or independent media can sustain a sport beyond 'cottage' level is highly dubious. This is an especially important question that has a key influence on parallel issues of cause and effect regarding which sports might flourish and which are unlikely to succeed. This is not a simple matter of particular sports being made successful by media, especially by television coverage.

While media may stimulate interest in sports (such as basketball during the 1990s) and construct competitions with a physical dimension (such as *The Amazing Race*), the kind of long-term, dedicated participant and spectator foundation required for sports to be both large-scale and sustainable cannot be readily conjured up by the media.

Similarly, 'folk' sport and other cultural practices may persist with negligible or intermittent media coverage. However, the media are crucial to the professional and commercial flourishing of sport because they simultaneously cater to, and fuel, popular interest in it, while also providing much of the capital infrastructure, through television broadcast rights, that enables it to survive and develop as an industrial enterprise.

Thus, the media, especially television, produce their own hierarchy of sports that is self-sustaining and has profound implications for the relative position of those sports. A large international survey of the sports press conducted in 2005 (encompassing 10,007 articles in the sports pages of 37 newspapers in 10 countries)discovered that the print media cover, with some national variation, a very narrow range of mainly male sports (Schultz-Jorgensen, 2005).

There is, unsurprisingly, considerable overlap between print and broadcast media as to which sports are heavily privileged (Rowe, 2004a), irrespective of whether newspapers or television stations have common owners (although, of course, there are clear connections between sporting priorities within a single media company). If an Australian component (in which I was involved) of the international survey of the sports press is appraised, it can be seen that there is a high concentration on a small range of sports in the press, and that this pattern confers an enormous advantage on those sports in determining the profile, and so commercial position, of these sports.

The survey consisted of a content analysis of the sports pages of selected newspapers over 14 consecutive weeks from April 11th until July 24th 2005, alternating the day sampled every week (for this reason, predictable factors like seasonality, as well as extraordinary events such as corruption or athlete sexual assault scandals, should be regarded as actually or potentially affecting the findings)[1].

In Australia, the sports pages of the *Sydney Morning Herald* (a major metropolitan broadsheet newspaper owned by the Fairfax company); the *Australian* and the *Herald Sun* (respectively a national broadsheet and a Melbourne-based metropolitan tabloid newspaper, both owned by Rupert Murdoch's News Corporation); and the *West Australian* (a tabloid regional newspaper based in Perth that is independently owned) were subjected to content analysis in the sample period.

The total number of articles for the four newspapers in the sample period was 1,131 sports articles, of which 330 were in the *Sydney Morning Herald.* The main sports represented in the *Sydney Morning Herald* sample are presented in Table I below:

Table I: Most Frequently Represented Sports in the* Sydney Morning Herald *by Article in the Sample Period

Sport	*Percentage of articles*	*Number of articles*
Rugby League	23.6	78
Rugby Union	14.8	49
Australian Football	9.6	32
Association Football	9.3	31
Equestrian (including Racing)	9.1	30
Cricket	8.5	28
Tennis	5.5	18
Golf	4.2	14
Other Motor Sports	3.3	11

It can be seen from the data presented above that almost 90 per cent of sports articles in the *Sydney Morning Herald*in the sample periodwas devoted to just nine sports, with a single sport (rugby league) approaching a quarter of all sports stories.

Correspondingly, several sports presented in the Table 2 had less than two per cent of all articles in the sports pages:

When the same calculation was made for all four Australian newspapers in total, there was, as can be seen in Table III below, considerable similarity in the patterns of coverage.

Variations can be explained by such factors as regional sport preferences (rugby league, for example, is much more popular in Sydney, New South Wales than in Melbourne, Victoria), while the reverse is the case with Australian Rules Football.

Table II: Sports in the* Sydney Morning Herald *by Article in the Sample Period with Less than 2 per cent of All Articles

Sport	Number of Articles
Boxing	6
Basketball	5
Cycling	5
Formula 1	4
Swimming	3
Netball	3
American Football	2
Squash	2
Track and Field	2
Baseball	1

Indeed, the sports of field hockey and gymnastics were not covered at all in the *Sydney Morning Herald* sample.

There are also socio-demographic variations in sports following (the *Sydney Morning Herald* covers extensively the socially elite sport of rugby union because it fits well with its targeted 'up-market' readership, whereas the targeted readership of the *Herald Sun* is further down the scale of social class, with corresponding variations in the pattern of cultural (including sport) taste preferences (Bennett *et. al.*, 1999).

Some sports are not only under-represented in the sports press but, at least in sampling terms, invisible (see Table IV) below.

Of course, the international sports press survey provided a framework that embraced sports that have great or little apparent appeal in various countries, and so reveals national taste preferences in sport through the sport media. Nordic and Alpine skiing, team handball and volleyball are much more popular in Europe than in other continents while, similarly, martial arts, table tennis and badminton are more prominent in Asia.

Table III: Sports with Articles over 2 Per Cent of the Total in All Four Newspapersby Article in the Sample Period

Sport	*Percentage of articles*	*Number of articles*
Australian Rules Football	30.8	348
Rugby League	14.8	167
Association Football	8.0	90
Equestrian (including Racing)	7.3	82
Rugby Union	7.0	79
Cricket	6.5	74
Tennis	5.6	63
Golf	4.2	48
Other Motor Sports	3.6	38
Basketball	2.1	24
Boxing	2.1	24

These data reveal that globalization in sport is by no means 'complete', given the wide variations in sport media coverage, participation and spectatorship, but they also suggest, as is supported by the full international survey, the ways in which different national media sport markets work in a highly concentrated way that generally favours male-dominated sports, and with a high level of collusion between sport journalists and the commercial sport industry (Schultz-Jorgensen, 2005).

Table IV: Sports Not Covered in the Sports Pages of All Four Newspapersin Australia in the Sample Period

- Sport
- Alpine Skiing
- Badminton
- Beach Volleyball
- Bodybuilding and Fitness Sports
- Canoe and Kayak

- Dancing (all kinds)
- Martial Arts
- Nordic Skiing
- Sailing (all kinds)
- Table Tennis
- Team Handball
- Volleyball

The extent to which these patterns of media sport coverage are self-evidently the product of sporting popularity, and the degree do they establish a circular feedback loop, whereby intensive media coverage stimulates and reproduces sporting popularity, should be keenly debated, especially when one key measure of a specific sport's standing is media coverage itself.

Indeed, within as well as between countries, sports with substantial levels of participation and spectatorship are often not well represented in the media. Here other questions, such as gender, come into play (Creedon, 1994; Rowe, 2005;Scraton and Flintoff, 2002) which are not the main subject of this paper, but must be prominent in any analysis of sports power structures, including in the discussion of sport celebrity below.

In the context of this discussion, the next matter to be addressed is the manner in which sports and sportspeople reach beyond the sport media and into the wider world of the entertainment media, where sporting celebrity is created across the wider culture, and thereby helps further to entrench particular sporting interests at the expense of others, and so reveals again the power of the media over and within sport.

Since the late 21st century the media have successfully turned sport stars who were once mainly 'local heroes' into global figures like basketballer Michael Jordan, whose visual image and name were once surveyed to be the most recognisable in the world (Andrews, 2001).

Sport and Celebrity

Sport tends to conceive of itself as the ultimate meritocracy, with the clear measures of success and failure in open competition providing the kind of transparency that is rarely apparent in other types of business or, indeed, in politics (despite their analogous measures of financial or electoral fortune).

In the sport world, then, talent, diligence and motivation should operate in combination to enable sportspeople to be sorted into reliable hierarchies, with team sports introducing additional complexities of group and interpersonal cohesion.

Setting aside the aberrant phenomena of corruption (such as bribery) and cheating (such as the use of performance-enhancing drugs), the deep involvement of the media, advertising and commercial sponsorship in sport creates the circumstances whereby the success of individual sportspeople and teams is substantially the product of non-sporting factors.

Thus, it might be asked, 'are sport celebrities the best in the business, or the best for business?'

As noted above, the media contribute to and even construct a sports order. Within sports, calculations are also made concerning the 'saleability' of sportspeople in relation to qualities that may not reflect actual sporting performance.

It can, of course, be argued that professional sport is not just about performance on the field of play. This is undoubtedly correct – sport is of no intrinsic worth, and, if its major justification is its contribution to the nation's health, it is a rather inefficient and eccentric form of exercise. As physical culture sport can be aesthetically pleasing, but often quite ugly, and the sports narrative can be compelling, but only erratically so.

The principal motor behind professional sport is passionate, largely irrational fandom (Horne *et. al.*, 1999) but media sport culture has flourished by moving well beyond this base to connect with more diverse constituencies for whom sport may be of little more than passing interest, or which may attract attention for reasons that have little to do with sport.

From a commercial point of view this is a logical development – sport stars are merely one form of 'talent' that can be promoted and sold in the same way as television actors and pop singers. But, just as acting and musical talent are often subjugated by other forms of appeal, sporting performance can recede in importance, displaced by marketing strategies and image manufacture.

Thus, sport and exercise professionals need to consider their role in the production and reproduction of celebrity in sport, and the extent to which they may be, intentionally or otherwise, implicated in such processes. The media sport marketplace does not only favour a concentration on certain sports, but also on particular sports organizations and people (Andrews and Jackson, 2001; Whannel, 2001).

Thus, a celebrity system has been created that has created a series of 'brands'. These may be peak sport bodies (such as FIFA, IOC), clubs and teams (Real Madrid, Manchester United, Chicago Bulls) and, with variable relationships to the above organizations, individual stars (Michael Jordan, Tiger Woods, David Beckham, Yao Ming).

The appeal of a star is preferably that they are unquestionably the best performers in their given sports, but this is not the main criterion and is neither a necessary nor sufficient condition for achieving sport celebrity. There are many other variables, including the intensity of the marketing and promotion campaigns behind them; their capacity to operate effectively at both national and global levels; their ability to sell other products and services, including their own image; and something less tangible and predictable – the capacity to capture the *Zeitgeist* (spirit of the times).

Sport celebrity, then, is produced at the intersection of athleticism, industry, image manufacture and cultural momentum.

The complex construction of the sporting elite makes it difficult to disentangle cause and effect in sport 'ranking', and so problematises the principles on which esteem, status and reward in contemporary sport are based. As Ellis Cashmore (2002: 164) notes in his book devoted to the 'phenomenon' of the prominent footballer David Beckham:

> *Whether or not Beckham is a charismatic genius touched by greatness isn't my real concern; this book isn't about whether he deserves such a transcendent label. Or whether his talent is exaggerated. He creates electrifying football on the field; but he too has been created. Created by a fandom, wide and variegated, and infinitely generous in its acclaim. Assisted by a calculating, efficient publicity apparatus, Beckham has been afforded a status beyond the grasp of the merely talented. The kinds of qualities, perhaps gifts, he's thought to possess have propelled him into spheres unknown to previous generations of footballers, and even contemporary players of comparable if not greater technical ability.*

Isolating this sportsman's qualities from the " calculating, efficient publicity apparatus" that feeds into a voracious media machine is a near impossible task. Beckham's current and previous clubs, Manchester United and Real Madrid, both have their own television channels, with the latter now broadcasting inter-continentally via satellite on a digital platform.

A key aspect of this branding exercise involves the sale of television subscriptions and merchandising in relatively unexploited Asian markets. This strategy has not only involved broadcasting European sports events in Asia, but, via the aforementioned NICL, it has entailed attracting Asian sportsmen to 'mature' media sport markets overseas in order to infuse them with new consumers from populous, economically developing countries.

Thus, apart from their obvious sporting talent, Korean footballers like Park Ji-Sung and Lee Young Pyo playing English Premier League football, or basketballer Yao Ming in the USA's National Basketball Association (NBA), bring substantial economic benefit through new spectatorship.

Indeed, it has been suggested that in some cases player recruitment has been made on the basis of the lucrative enlistment of fans from their country of origin. Thus, Wilson (2005: n.p.) has noted in relation to association football, "in Scotland, Celtic have admitted they partly bought Japanese player Shunsuke Nakamura for the 'opportunities he will bring in terms of commercial spin-offs, especially in Japan and the Far East'", quoting Cannon's remark that "clubs have their eyes on four potential prizes: new sponsorship deals, match fees, merchandising opportunities, and overseas TV rights".

Off-season tours by European football clubs to Asia and America, coupled with sponsorship deals like Chelsea's with Samsung, Everton's (Chang Beer), Manchester United's (Vodafone) and Arsenal's (Emirates), are pivotal components of the sport celebrity system.

Securing such resources has the structural effect of separating sports, clubs, teams and athletes into a small, transnationally oriented elite and a much larger group of locally focused and much less affluent organizations and individuals. Sport and exercise professionals are, similarly, distributed across this growing divide.

The powerful commercial forces that construct sport celebrity have a distorting effect not only on who prospers in sport, but what constitutes 'success' in sport. For example, it was noted above that sport remains male-dominated, especially in team games. But it is possible for women to be prominent and very well remunerated, especially in the more affluent professional individual sports such as tennis and golf. One traditional way of achieving attention and reward for sportswomen that highlights the fusion of sport and entertainment is the projection of a sexualised image that has little in common with sporting performance (Hargreaves, 1994; Messner, 2002).

Probably the best-known example of sport celebrity created through sexuality rather than high performance is that of the now-retired Anna Kournikova, who garnered media coverage (Harris and Clayton, 2002) out of all proportion to her status as a tennis player who has never one a major singles tournament.

Yet, through sponsorships and endorsements of companies like adidas, Yonex, and Omega, and Berlei, and appearing in men's magazines such as *Maxim* and *Loaded*, Kournikova has been more visible and better remunerated than many women players who have been more successful on court (by 2002, at the age of 21, she had earned over US$40m). Indeed, in the 2001 season, Kournikova earned only US$334,000 actually playing tennis, just over 3 per cent of a total income of US$10.6 million (Hooper, 2002). Kournikova's relative failure as a player (in terms of her financial rewards) did cause her sponsors concern, revealing that sport celebrities are ultimately expected to excel at their chosen sports discipline, but her case also indicated that celebrity can be achieved (if not sustained) in sport without peak performance (Smart, 2005).

In sport, as with other zones of celebrity, fame, conspicuousness and reward may be dynamic, unstable and unpredictable. For example, Korean American golfer Michelle Wie has attracted considerable sporting and commercial interest after turning professional in 2005 just before her sixteenth birthday, and the trajectory of her career is as yet unclear. But with large sponsorship contracts with Nike and Sony, she instantly became the world's highest earning female golfer and third highest earning sportswoman in the world after tennis players Maria Sharapova and Serena Williams (BBC, 2005). Those with an intimate or passing involvement in sport might legitimately ponder such exposures of the workings of the media sports cultural complex.

Conclusion

The intention of this paper is not to induce cynicism among sport and exercise professionals. To do so would be futile and self-defeating, because sport is an important element of contemporary culture that does offer many benefits for participants and spectators (some of whom are the same people, or who switch roles at various stages of the life cycle). As David Andrews (2006: 270) argues:

> *Sport's tacit visceral physicality, dramatic uncertainty, and subjective interpellation make it a compelling and seductive aspect of popular existence for both spectators and participants alike.*

Sport is, then, physical culture, popular pleasure and service industry, and it can hardly be insulated from the material world in the manner proposed by its own mythologies.

Thus, those with professional and affective investments in sport – in many cases these are one and the same - must come to terms with the major processes described above that shape contemporary society and the world of sport within it that, in turn, exerts its influence on that society at global and national levels. Instead of ascribing to these processes the power of 'unstoppability', it is possible to intervene in the formal and informal politics of sport, rather than submit to a sense of resignation at the inevitability of it all.

A vital prerequisite of understanding sport in order to improve it is the recognition of the power of the media in sport, and of media sports culture within the social formation.

It makes little sense to advocate the 'de-mediatization' of sport – as noted above, without the media, sport would not be the socio-cultural force that it has become, and would remain largely a part of pre-industrial folk culture or the principal domain of the local physical artisans and craft workers of early modernity. For sport to return to earlier modalities would not only be anachronistic, it would also imply that a 'golden age' of sport once existed that has been extinguished by malign influences.

But the 'purity' of traditional sport is an illusion, with critical histories of sport offering strong evidence of commercialism, corruption and discrimination in earlier epochs (see, for example, Guttmann, 2004). The 'politics of acquisition' described in the title of this paper is one that revolves around the capacity to place sport's popularity in the service of many, diverse interests and agenda, especially by utilising the media's capacity to capture and relay messages ranging from which branded commodities to consume, to how one's own and other nations should be viewed (Wenner, 1998).

Effective interventions in this politics of sport should be based, in the first instance, on asking the awkward questions that are often left unasked in the face of the hyperbole surrounding contemporary sport:

- Why do some sports and sportspeople receive such apparently disproportionate rewards and attention at the expense of others?
- What is the role of the commercial media in creating and maintaining such sports hierarchies, and how, can conflicts of interest between sports organizations, sponsors and media be controlled?
- How can structural social inequalities of class, race, ethnicity and gender be resisted rather than reproduced in sport?
- In what ways can sport be democratised, enabling more people involved in it at all levels to shape its development, rather than leaving key decision-making in the hands of small clusters of sports administrators and corporate executives.

These are by no means new questions, but they are often submerged by currently dominant notions of maximising capital return, securing media profile, undermining the positions of competitors, and concealing or excusing the many negative phenomena in sport that continue to bedevil it.

These circumstances place a special responsibility on the sport and exercise professionals who can be expected to exercise guardianship of sport. In any occupation, it is often easier to accept the *status quo*, and to be reluctant to challenge entrenched institutional ideology and common wisdom.

Sport, with its powerful Olympian ideals and myths of transcendence, is particularly resistant to critical inquiry, because to confront its failings is often seen to betray a noble institution. By contrast, it can be strongly asserted that contemporary sport is in urgent need not of more public relations, but of greater public and professional scrutiny. Those who inhabit and operate its organizations, from the lowest to the highest strata, and from the training ground to the television studio, can surely lead rather than obstruct this project of sporting renewal from the heart of the media sports cultural complex itself.

Andrews, D. L. (2006) 'Introduction: Playing with the Pleasure Principle', *The South Atlantic Quarterly*. The sports and sporting goods industries have grown to become immensely influential and rich and one of the world largest industries. The power of sport for development, conflict prevention and good health is also a major force. Media companies and journalists have a central role to play as a pillar of democratic market economies. They face higher expectations for ethical and responsible practices as an influential part of the global business community which is not exempt from distrust and pressures for greater transparency. He outlines a range of measures that a responsible media company can take to maintain standards and be a force for good development, and outlines how affordable access to low cost technologies have introduced a new countervailing force for democracy and activism.

Sport and the Media must surely be the most potent combination of forces amongst the key actors in the globalisation game. They have a unique synergy sport as the premier global media content, and media as the premier partner for sport and sports industries. A result of this alliance applied to the worlds most attractive activity is immense audiences, immense economic influence and power, and immense reach into countries and communities. If conducted openly, responsibly and in the public good it also brings immense potential for helping create in the long-term a more healthy, understanding, inclusive and stable world.

But the commercial world of media and sport is full of IFS. I would like to reflect on how sport has risen to become one of the worlds leading and most powerful industries. What are the implications for society which is increasingly concerned with corporate social responsibility and corporate citizenship ? What is the role of the professional journalist on the front line of these immense commercial empires inter-facing with politics, powerful stars and brands ? And how could the media be a force for good in sports development in a troubled world of increasing risk youth unemployment and conflict ?

I speak from the perspective of having worked for over a decade with international and multinational companies, including some of the largest media companies, sports sponsors and some sporting goods producers, promoting corporate citizenship, the engagement of business in bringing solutions to social problems through partnerships for development in over 50 countries around the world.

There has seldom been a time when global risks and dangers have been accompanied by so many opportunities. Sports industries, and all associated with them the professional and amateur clubs and athletes, the sporting goods industries, and the massive ancillary world of travel, communications and sports sponsors have an enormous and positive potential role to play in many of the key issues of engagement, reduction of corruption, conflict and sustainability that we face in the world today.

First - How has sport risen to become one of the worlds leading and most powerful industries ?

There is in my view too little recognition of how the business of sport, at community, national and international level, both recreational and professional, can be a positive force for good health, peace, development and ethics in a world that is hungry for values. Even those in the sports industries may not yet, in my view, have come to terms with the influence they now have, and can have, due to the emergence of globalisation and the many threats and challenges which now arise.

Sport plays a unique part in our lives. After work itself it is the largest focus of mass civil participation. It has more voluntary community level leaders and teachers than any other human activity including religion. Together with related services it is the largest employer. It attracts the largest audiences of any activity on the planet. It consistently fills more pages in more newspapers, uniquely transcending geography, politics, class, race, sex, culture and religion.

It has many of the best-known and most potent global brands in sporting goods, sports teams and associated sponsors. It is populated by the best known celebrity personalities. It is the subject of the worlds highest value TV and communications deals, and the highest priced advertising slots the TV rights to the last Soccer World Cup and Olympic Games combined were reported as being over $2.3 billion (thats 40 cents for everyone on the planet). It can also be a trigger for urban development through regeneration lead by sports developments as we have seen in many inner city areas.

Sport business is also very big. The sporting goods industries alone are estimated to have an annual retail market possibly of over $600 billion, linked to a global network of small and big businesses, focussed primarily on the 16 to 25 age group - which is more than the GDP of many countries.

This doesnt count in media revenues and sponsorship, travel and tourism, infrastructure, associated food and beverages, gambling, corporate entertaining, and millions from sports club and entrance fees. European soccer leagues alone are said to be a $10 billion market. Like few other industries, it has from the start exploited the potential of globalisation, and has been at the forefront of internationalisation for almost a century. And yet, uniquely, and with the exception of activist campaigns against some branded goods, it has escaped the storm of public protest now associated with almost all other aspects of globalisation.

Sport also has a major role to play in the world due to critical problems of health and increasing rates of non-communicable disease linked to diet and lack of physical activity which according to the WHO is fast becoming the main health danger worldwide. It also has a critical part to play in conflict prevention and in economic development, particularly amongst young people.

It is not surprising that sport, in spite of much publicised soccer hooliganism, has been a medium for vital and pioneering peaceful contact between East and West, Hindu and Muslim, across the religious divides in Northern Ireland or heralding in ping-pong matches the opening of China in the late 1960s.

It has suspended conflict in the no-mans-land between the First World War trenches, refugee camps in the Balkans, between Capitalism and Communism during the Cold War, between the North and South Koreas of today and no doubt, if politicians made way to more willing human spirits, in the Middle East tomorrow.

Sport can underpin and celebrate diversity. A common language we have with the people of Israel, Palestine, Jordan and Iraq is the language of soccer ! Sport is a powerful neutraliser with an accepted global language and global rules. It can be an important twin track in global diplomacy

Sport must be a critical potential component of development in a world where some three billion people live on less than $2 a day, or amongst the unemployed on our own door-steps. Helping build communities, develop young people, reduce risks of conflict, and contribute to good health are critical building blocks of development.

Sport and its values of fitness, fair play and participation has a unique part to play in a troubled world. The shocking events of doping scandals, Olympic bribery and corruption, of the past year since the 11th September, and also the crisis of confidence caused by corporate governance scandals, have all brought home to us all how fragile, small and vulnerable our inter-connected world is and how important trust is. Also how these far off global issues are now on our doorstep, and how according to reliable attitude surveys our stakeholders consumers, investors, employees, regulators, media and the public in general are wanting values based leadership.

Secondly, why should social responsibility be of concern to the Media ? And what is the role of the professional journalist on the front line of these immense commercial empires inter-facing with politics, powerful stars and brands ?

The media has a uniquely important part to play in functioning democracy and open market economies as a vital check and balance on abuse of political and economic power. Journalists themselves, who protect their editorial freedom fiercely, at least in many countries, are rightly proud and protective of their professional ethics. But then it gets complicated.

I think it is necessary to distinguish here between journalists and media companies they work for, who have different interests and are subject to other forces. It is also necessary to recognize there are questions of content that sometimes create tensions through the need to sell copy, sell newspapers, attract viewers and command advertising on the one hand and the duty to explain, analyse, reveal and respect on the other.

The survey conducted by MandagMorgan Industry or Independence ?: survey of the Scandinavian sports press confirms a trend that others have observed in the media around the world of almost a race to the bottom in terms of superficial content in sports coverage focusing on personalities, events and gossip rather than much if any serious content, and almost nothing on the political, economic and social aspects of sport.

Commenting on the lack of critical enquiry into sports affairs a media analyst from the Research Institute for Sport, Culture and Civil Society describes how \"a kind of holy trinity exists between media, the professional sports clubs and money interests\".

All too often media companies claim editorial freedom when questioned on lack of inquiry by their papers or broadcasting stations into sensitive areas, or lack of interest in low quality standards. It seems to many extraordinary that commercial advertisers are subjected to more rigorous standards of decency and honesty in most countries, and subject to greater scrutiny, yet the tabloid text alongside the advert may carry innuendo, half-truth and misrepresentation defended as editorial freedom.

Some journalists attempting to cover broader issues of sport, including doping and bribery scandals, economic interests and corruption in the sports world have faced ridicule, intimidation, censorship and dismissal before their stories proved sound.

Media and communications companies are part of the mainstream international commercial business community. This past decade has seen the issues of corporate social responsibility move increasingly rapidly from the fringe of management practice of a few pioneers, some of them in your industries, to a major issue for the Boardroom agenda. In the process it has attracted increasing attention and widespread public interest, and is now seen by many institutions, from the United Nations, World Bank, European Union, and OECD down, as a key part of the solution to pressing governance and development challenges.

The media has played key roles in exposing bad ethical practice, scandals, vested interests and double standards whether in business or in personalities. But the media often faces criticisms of putting events, personalities, entertainment, gossip and sensationalism I guess what makes the news ahead of the need to explain context, take a more analytical view and look at issues in the longer-term way that solutions to complex issues and progress require.

Then there is the problem of patronage and marketing deals for exclusive rights, often overpriced as we have recently seen in the cases of collapsed European media organizations, to compliant bidders in a sellers market. The media as commercial organizations, and organizations prosper on access to critical events and stars whether valuable World Cup rights, access to lucrative Chinese markets, access to exclusive Presidential and Prime Ministerial press briefings or ringside seats in the amphitheatres of War. They also recognize where their interests lie in avoiding provocative action that may make them vulnerable to being excluded from access to a deal or privileged briefing opportunity, even if temporarily, and thus loose competitive advantage to other media companies. By and large media companies as businesses are cautious, show risk adverse behavior and have a herd instinct.

In spite of its critical role as a pillar or democracy, trust in the media is not that high, and generally lower than trust in the armed forces, NGOs and Government. A recent survey by Gallup International and Environics International for the World Economic Forum the Voice of the People Survey (July-September 2002) of 36,000 people across 47 countries - suggests that trust has fallen to critical proportions.

Overall some 69% put some or a lot of trust in the armed forces compared with 26% who put little or no trust. NGOs score 59% trust, the UN 52%, religious institutions and the police each score 57%. Government scores 50% and press and the media 49%, with 47% showing little or no trust in the media.

The legal system, global and national companies and Parliaments were the only institutions scoring lower on little or no trust compared to the media. In North America and Europe the media was consistently trusted less then Governments, except where it was more trusted in Asia, Latin America, Africa and the Middle East.

Put simply, Corporate Social Responsibility is the framework for the role of business in society - it is the set of standards of behaviour to which a company subscribes in order to make its impact on society positive and productive. The production and selling of goods and services, business ethics, environmental practices, recruitment and employment conditions, approach to human rights and investment in the community are examples of such impact. Globally the media is dominated by some 10 companies and 50 sub-regional companies.

MEDIA SPORTS INVESTMENTS

Media Sports Investments (M.S.I.) is an international fund of investors and was registered as a company in London on 31 August 2004 with Iranians Kia Joorabchian and Nojan Bedroud listed as directors in filings at Companies House.

Rumours persist over the involvement of Russian Oligarchs Roman Abramovich and Boris Berezovsky behind the scenes of MSI, with Chelsea FC owner Abramovich reputedly owning a 15% share of the investment group.

Corinthians signed a controversial deal with MSI in 2004 that grants the company a large degree of control of the club, in exchange for large investments. The deal lasts for 10 years. This has brought many players to the team, such as former Boca Juniors star Carlos Tévez, midfielders Marcelo Mattos, Gustavo Nery, Roger, Javier Mascherano and Carlos Alberto, and defenders Sebastián Domínguez and Marinho, as well as coaches Passarella, Márcio Bittencourt and Antonio Lopes.

At the beginning of the 2005-06 season, MSI was behind an attempt by Kia Joorabchian to take over English club West Ham United. The plan was officially abandoned in November of the same year, when agreement on a valuation of the club could not be reached.

On 31 August 2006, Kia Joorabchian's involvement with Corinthians looked to have resulted in the club's biggest stars, Javier Mascherano & Carlos Tevez, being loaned out to West Ham; instead it was confirmed that West Ham had in fact signed the players on a permanent deal, not a loan basis. All other details of the transfers were not disclosed. On September 1, 2006, the day after Javier Mascherano & Carlos Tevez made a permanent move to West Ham, the club announced the opening of "exploratory discussions" over a possible takeover, reportedly by a consortium fronted by Joorabchian and Paul Yeubrey. Discussions ended with the confirmation on 21 November 2006 that Eggert Magnússon had succeeded in a rival bid for the East London club.

After the fall of Corinthians to the Brazilian Championship's second division, in 2 December, 2007, the ex-coach of the team, Antonio Lopes said that MSI was not responsible for that. "There was no sequence to the 2005 Brazilian championship title", said Lopes.

Also after the fall of Corinthians to the Brazilian Championship's second division, Joorabchian denied any kind of responsibility on that. He said it was other people's fault such as his rival, the Brazilian coach Emerson Leão.

4

Air Heads

PARAGLIDING - SPORT OR OBSESSION ?

The dream of free flight has always been with us. Many extreme sports these days are all trying to somehow simulate the notion of flight. These range from maddening mountain bike down hills with huge drops en route, to jumping off cliffs on snowboards and skis. What is so appealing to the notion of experiencing the pull of gravity, and hurtling one self through the air, all for the sake of achieving those minuscule moments of being truly airborne?

Yet, there is one sport which has captivated the hearts of those that wanted to experience the closest thing to being an actual bird. This is the sport of paragliding. It does not just give one that free, floating feeling for mere seconds as bunji jumping might, or going further even, base jumping. Paragliding lets you actually fly and achieve something that comes closest to being a real bird, and in a sense, a true modern day's Icarus.

Air Heads is a documentary film which examines the subculture of paragliding. Following in the footsteps of cult classics like Canada's National Film board's *"Ski Bums"* or the Surf epics *"Endless Summer" ormore recently " Riding Giants "*, Airheads examines people with an obsession for flying. What makes this film special is the fact that as of yet, besides short lived cult industry flicks, there has not been a proper, general interest documentary, ever done on the sport.

"What exactly is paragliding? ", one may ask. It involves running off a mountainside with an already inflated parachute like device. It is often confused with the sport of parasailing, or being towed by a motorboat. Others often mistake it for skydiving or parachuting itself.

Paragliding has an interesting but fairly recent history. The filmmakers will follow the sport from it's inception. It is rumoured to have begun in a small French town in the Alps, back in 1985. In those days, the nouveau flyers discovered that by running down a mountainside with an open parachute, one could lift them, and actually accomplish a short flight.

Since then as technology progressed, the older parachute like devices have been replaced by elaborate, modern contraptions which resemble more the shape of a wing. What makes this all fascinating is the sport is so new it is still constantly changing, progressing and developing as we learn and try to keep up with it.

But it is the people as always which make this sport such an interesting phenomenon.

Air Heads will examine a variety of colourful characters obsessed with this new concept of soaring. Among these, the viewers will meet people including; Jim and Corrine Orava. Jim, from Pemberton BC and French/Swiss born Corrine, 28 met and were soon married after an encounter at a paragliding event in France. Jim, a stuntman and rigger in the film business is a champion paraglide pilot.

Corrine has been flying since her teenage years in Europe where the sport has accelerated with unsurpassed velocity. Since then, the couple have travelled the world, flying in Turkey, Peru, Venezuela, Romania, Nepal, to the Dominican Republic.

Having made their home in Pemberton, BC, they enjoy a flying location in their back yard which rivals some of the best soaring in the world, right off their Mt McKenzie launch site. They have also accumulated a wealth of footage from their travels.

Then, of course is Lars Taylor. Lars was an Olympic athlete having competed on Canada's national cross country ski team back in 1991. After a mountain biking accident Lars became a paraplegic and wheelchair bound. He has since married and taken up paragliding in his wheelchair. He and his wife are both certified pilots and she often assists him by pushing him down the takeoff ramp.

Ptor Spricenieks is a minimalist in life. Known to many as a ski mountaineer and big mountain extreme skier, Ptor has taken on paragliding as extension of his being. Ptor lives the simple good life, often working a garden on a patch of land, or subsidising his being with a bit of carpentry. It is Ptor's spiritual beliefs which link his flying to his life adventures. Living small, acting big was always his fortey. Ptor's achievements include a first ski descent of Mt Robson's North Face.

Consider Sonja Cameron, an attractive twenty some young woman who is hooked on the sport. Sonja is an avid scuba diver and compares the feeling of weightlessness between the two sports.

Chris Kettles is a climber, ski mountaineer who has since taken up flying as an extension to his love for the mountains. He flies as often as he can in Pemberton with his good friend Ptor Spricenieeks with whom they often philosophise about spiritual beliefs and the karmic chill which paragliding offers them both. Chris has networked, organized and co-ordinated many trips and expeditions in the Pemberton/Whistler community and was a well remembered character in ski bums.

Chris Muller, 28 is the top gun hanglider and paraglide pilot based in Cochrane, Alberta. Chris holds many international paraglide and hangliding records following in the footsteps of his dad, Willi Muller, who died paragliding some time back. To this day there is a Muller challenge held out of Golden BC in the honour of his dad who pioneered the sport of hangliding in Canada.

Asia Siwocha, 38 is an attractive, athletic mother of two. After her first tandem flight she had tears in her eyes from the exhilaration experienced by her first flight. The film will follow Asia's quest to learn how to fly as she joins the ranks of the Air Heads. She wants to share this feeling with her kids and will be taking her seven year old daughter tandem together with another pilot.

Rounding up the team is Peter Chrzanowski, 46, an adventure filmmaker who has been flying for 15 years but only this year experienced the thrill of thermal flying. Peter is a character study in himself as far as his long list of filming mountaineering accomplishments as well as accidents go. Now he ventures head long into the sport again, this time both as a paragliding aficionado as well as a filmmaker. Peter will be flying and filming while homesteading on a property below Pemberton's McKenzie launch next door to Chris, something which will provide additionally colourful content.

Going still further in their addiction to flying, we will hear stories of people leaving their spouses or losing loved ones as they seek that ultimate thermal lift.

"Dangerously Easy "perhaps comes to mind best, when describing the sport. It's easy to learn but also easy to get cocky, thus ending up killed.

Stories of paragliders hitting hundred foot tall Cedar trees, getting sucked into Thunder head clouds, or having terrifying wing collapses still dominate many fireside chats. Due to all this and more, Airheads becomes such an appropriate title to an obsession with a sport which demands such intense focus, that to so many, other things in life, become trivial and left unintentionally behind. Many of these occurrences can be re-enacted.

Technology as well, has accelerated the sport towards unprecedented performance. The earlier wings only had a four to one glide ratio, while the new paragliders boast an unprecedented eight to one ratio. This enables the modern day's pilots to stay in the air for hours and even travel huge distances, catching thermals and flying hundreds of kilometres, along mountainous ridges or scalding deserts. All this, while precariously suspended by a few meagre strings, hanging in the heavens from a nylon canopy. Since then paragliders have launched off Everest and have made top landings on peaks such as Europe's highest Mt Blanc.

Airheads will capitalize not only on great stories and magnificent visuals, but it will also dwell into the psychology of human behaviour examining some of our addiction to the adrenaline of flight. There will be stories told, stories recounted as well as just some great reality moments as the characters all interact in, sometimes, the most precautious situations. Sometimes sad, sometimes extremely funny, the film will examine our fascination with this phenomenon.

5

Climate Change and Winter Sports

INTRODUCTION

For many alpine areas winter sports are the most important source of income, and snow-reliability is one of the key elements of the touristic offers. Skiing and snowboarding, but also snow related sports such as cross-country skiing or snow hiking depend on enough snow.

Mountain areas are sensitive to climate change. Implications of climate change can be seen, for example, in less snow, receding glaciers, melting permafrost and more extreme events like landslides.

Furthermore, climate change will shift mountain flora and fauna. Second order impacts will occur in mountain agriculture, mountain hydropower and, of course, mountain tourism.

However, climate change is a severe threat to snow related sports such as skiing, snowboarding and cross-country skiing. Lower earnings in winter tourism will reinforce economic disparities between urban areas and the less developed alpine regions.

Additionally, the ski tourism industry will "climb" up the mountains to reach snow reliable areas at high altitude. This process will lead to a concentration of winter sport activities, and will put further pressure on the sensitive environment of high mountains.

Clearly, it should be emphasised that climate is only one of many factors influencing snow tourism. However, less snow threatens the winter tourism industry in mountain areas.

Good snow conditions are a necessity, although that is not the only prerequisite for a financially viable mountain cableway company. Without enough snow, however, profitable ski tourism will scarcely be possible.

Mountains without snow are like summer without a sea. Apart from having sufficient snow at the right time - and particularly during the Christmas/New Year holidays - a key role is also played by the weather conditions (predominantly at the weekends). Since weekend and day guests are planning their trips at ever-shorter notice, it is not just the actual weather conditions that are a growing factor of influence, but the weather forecasts too.

Climate impact research on the winter tourism industry has been undertaken in various countries such as Canada, the U.S.A., Australia, New Zealand, Austria, Switzerland, France and the U.K. (see Koenig 1998 or Buerki 2000 for an overview).

All these studies show severe implications for the winter tourism industry if climate change were to occur. While some regions may be able to maintain their winter tourism with suitable, but expensive adaptation strategies (e.g. artificial snowmaking), others would lose their winter tourism industry due to a diminishing snow pack.

Global mean temperature has increased by about 0.6 - 1°C over the last 100 years (IPCC 2001). The years at the end of the nineties were the warmest over the last centuries.

Global temperature will increase in the future. Of course, there are a lot of uncertainties and the range of scenarios of the future warming is quite big. However, IPCC estimates a temperature increase of 1.4 to 5.8° until 2100. Global warming will be stronger on land surface, the northern hemisphere and in winter: that is the location and the season of mountain winter tourism.

CLIMATE CHANGE AND POTENTIAL IMPACTS ON WINTER TOURISM

Snow

The financial viability of the winter tourism industry depends on sufficient snow conditions. It was the winters with little snow at the end of the Eighties (1987/88 – 1989/90) that caused a stir in the Alps. The big difference to the situations at earlier periods with little snow is that the capital intensity of ski tourism had considerably increased. However, the most important link between climate change and mountain tourism is less snow and, as a consequence, less earnings in ski tourism.

Glaciers

There is a measured increase in the retreat of glaciers all over the world. Since 1850, Swiss Glaciers have lost more than a quarter of their surface. In 2030, 20 to 70% of Swiss glàciers will have disappeared. This is not only a severe lost of mountain aesthetic, but also a problem for ski slopes on glaciers in winter and summer skiing.

Permafrost

Global warming increases melting of permafrost and makes many mountain areas vulnerable to landslides. Mountain cableway stations, lift masts and other buildings in permafrost soil become instable. To brace and to anchor such buildings in melting permafrost-soils causes high costs. However, warming in mountain areas also makes hiking and climbing more dangerous due to increasing rockfall.

Changing Weather Conditions

On the one hand, the future climate will be warmer, on the other hand, the future climate will change its pattern. More precipitation or a higher fog level will lead to new conditions for mountain summer tourism such as hiking, trekking or biking. More and stronger extreme events are another threat for tourism activities and tourism infrastructure. Besides, with warmer winter temperatures ice fishing would be increasingly impossible.

CLIMATE CHANGE AND SNOW-DEFICIENT WINTERS

Results from the Alps

The economy in alpine regions is highly dependent on tourism. If the assumptions of the impacts of climate change hold true, snow cover in the Alps will diminish which will, in turn, jeopardise the tourism industry. The crucial factor for the long-term survival of mountain cableway companies is the frequency and regularity of winters with good snow conditions, or, put the other way round, the number of snow-deficient winters that can be withstood. It is not possible to give a definitive answer here, since the economic situation of the companies varies too much. The experience acquired by various ski resorts, however, shows that a ski resort can be considered snow-reliable if, in 7 out of 10 winters, a sufficient snow covering of at least 30 to 50 cm is available for ski sport on at least 100 days between December 1 and April 15.

Today, 85% of Switzerland's 230 ski resorts can be considered to be snow-reliable (tab. 1). However, even today a lot of ski resorts in the Prealps are not snow-reliable. If the line of snow-reliability were to rise to 1'500 m as a result of climate change (year 2030 – 2050), the number of snow-reliable ski resorts would drop to 63%. The Jura, Eastern and Central Switzerland, Ticino, and the Alps in the cantons of Vaud and Fribourg will be particularly jeopardised by global warming.

The ski regions of Valais and the Grisons will experience virtually no major problems, since the mean altitude of the cableway terminals in these regions is higher than 2500 m above sea level. If the line of snow-reliability were to rise to 1800 m, which is a possible scenario, there would be a further serious deterioration in conditions: only 44% of skiing regions could be designated as snow-reliable.

Even in the cantons of Grisons and Valais, approximately a quarter of the ski resorts would no longer be snow-reliable.

Table 1: Snow-reliability of Swiss ski resorts (Buerki 2000)

Region	Number of ski resorts	1200 masl No.	%	Snow-reliability 1500 masl No.	%	1800 masl No.	%
Jura	15	4	27	1	7	0	0
Alps (Vaud + Frib.)	19	16	84	7	37	4	21
Valais	54	54	100	52	96	40	74
Bern (ex. Jura)	35	30	86	20	57	12	34
Central Switzerland	35	26	74	13	37	7	20
Ticino	8	8	100	3	38	2	25
Eastern Switzerland	18	11	61	6	33	3	17
Grisons	46	46	100	42	91	33	72
Switzerland	230	195	85	144	63	101	44

A survey among tourists shows, that skiers will respond flexibly to changing snow conditions. During a period of snow-poor seasons, as expected more often under a changing climate, 49% of the skiers would change to a ski resort that is more snow-reliable. 32 % of the skiers would ski less often.

Although only 4% of the respondents would give up skiing, it can be concluded that climate change would have serious impacts on the number of skier days. The most vulnerable ski resorts in the lower regions of the Alps have to deal with a significant decrease of younger guests, day tourists and novice skiers, which is exactly the target group of these resorts (Buerki 2000).

The potential annual costs of climate change in Switzerland can be estimated at CHF 2.3 to 3.2 billion (US $ 1.5 to 2.1 billion) by the year 2050, which is 0.6 to 0.8% of the Swiss gross national product for 1995. CHF 1.8 to 2.3 billion (US $ 1.2 to 1.6 billion) would be accounted for by tourism. Even if there are many reservations that can be voiced regarding this calculation, it nevertheless shows that tourism is the economic sector that would be most affected by climate change in Switzerland and that this influence is of an order of magnitude that cannot be neglected.

Climate change will lead to a new pattern of favoured and disadvantaged ski tourism regions. If all other influencing factors remain the same, snow related sports would concentrate in the high-altitude areas that are snow-reliable in the future too. Ski resorts at lower altitudes will withdraw from the market sooner or later because of the lack of snow.

The only areas with good prospects will be those with transport facilities that provide access to altitudes higher than 2000 m. The regions at higher altitudes may experience greater demand, prompting a further expansion in quantitative terms. The pressure on ecologically sensitive high-mountain regions will increase.

The call for ski resorts with snow-reliability is the main argument for the current boom in concept studies to open up high mountain regions, or, in other words, climate change is the reason for opening up high mountain regions to tourism. In Switzerland more than 100 projects exist to extend ski sport infrastructure, a lot of them sponsored by subsidies. In the Alps as a whole, there are at least 300 projects, including, for example, new lifts, snow machines (including water reservoirs) and flattened slopes.

The impacts of climate change on winter tourism may be even more severe in countries such as Germany (for example resorts in the Black Forest area or in Allgaeu) and Austria, due to the lower altitudes of their ski resorts. The famous tourist town of Kitzbuehel, for example, lies at the low altitude of 760 m. In Austria, the present snow line will rise 200 to 300 metres higher with climatic change in the next 30 to 50 years. Many mountain villages, above all in the central and eastern parts of Austria, will lose their winter tourist industry because of climate change (Breiling & Charamza 1999).

In Italy, half of the winter sport villages are below 1,300 metres. Some of these are already facing major problems with snow cover. In future, there will only be a few winters with a winter atmosphere – that means with snow – in these ski resorts. If the altitude for snow reliability rises to 1,500m because of climatic change, winter sports would only be possible in the higher zones of the ski areas and many resorts would have no economic viability in the future.

However, the winter of 1998/99, in particular, February 1999, showed that the possibility of winters with a great deal of snow cannot be excluded in the future. In a study of the 'avalanche winter' of 1999, the direct losses incurred by mountain cable-ways as a result of avalanches and the large quantities of snow were estimated at CHF 15 million (US $ 10 million).

In total, 36 facilities were damaged, including 20 ski-lifts, 11 chair-lifts, 4 cable railways and 1 funicular. The mountain railway companies had to spend an extra 77% on snow clearing, compared with previous years. Roughly 25% more than in normal winters was spent on securing the ski slopes. All in all, the avalanche winter of 1999 probably caused losses in excess of CHF 200 million (US $ 130 million), the major portion of these having been indirect losses (SLF 2000).

Results from Australia

In order to find out how climate change may influence the snow-reliability of Australia's ski fields, impacts of different regional climate scenarios on the number of days with snow-cover were examined (Koenig 1998, tab. 2). Assuming the best-case scenario, all but one resort match the '60 days rule' in 2030. Assuming the worst-case scenario for 2030, a financially viable ski operation would only be possible in Charlotte Pass, but it would not be possible in three resorts at lower altitudes.

At all other resorts, ski operation would concentrate on the highest areas of today's ski fields, while top to bottom skiing would not be possible in most resorts. With the worst case scenario in 2070 none of today's ski resorts would be operating a profitable ski industry.

Table 2: Snow-reliability of Australian ski resorts (Koenig 1998)

Ski resort	'Best case' 2030 ? T= +0.3°C ? P= 0%	'Best case' 2070 ? T= +0.6°C ? P= 0%	'Worst case' 2030 ? T= +1.3°C ? P= -8%	'Worst case' 2070 ? T= +3.4°C ? P= -20%
Charlotte Pass	+	+	+	-
Thredbo	+	+	?/+	-
Perisher-Blue	+	+	?/+	-
Falls Creek	+	+	?/+	-
Hotham	+	+	?/+	-
Mt Buller	+	?/+	?	-
Mt Buffalo	+	?/+	-	-
Selwyn	+	?	-	-
Mt Baw Baw	-	-	-	-

(+) indicates that the prerequisite in terms of natural snow-cover duration for a financially viable ski operation (60 days rule) are accomplished.

(?) indicates that the prerequisite in terms of natural snow-cover duration for a financially viable ski operation are questionable.

(-) indicates that the prerequisite in terms of natural snow-cover duration for a financially viable ski operation are not accomplished.

"T = change of temperature; "P = change of precipitation

However, a concentration of the ski industry to the highest ski fields is expected due to climate change. Assuming today's snowmaking technology, the lower resorts would have to close down. In higher ski fields, where skiing would concentrate, expensive snowmaking might be intensified and environmental problems (waste water, rubbish) are likely to increase. This would undoubtedly result in conflicts with both conservation groups and the Australian Alpine National Parks.

Results from Canada

The impacts of climate change in Australia, Canada and the U.S.A. may be not as severe as in Europe because of the high level of artificial snowmaking. Recognising that snowmaking is an integral component of the ski industry the results indicate that ski areas could remain operational in a warmer climate, particularly within existing business planning and investment time horizons (into the 2020s) (Scott et al. 2003).

The economic impact of additional snowmaking requirements remains an important uncertainty. Under climate change scenarios and current snowmaking technology, the average ski season at the case study ski area in Canada (Lakelands tourism region) was projected to reduce by 0-16% in the 2020s, 7-32% in the 2050s and 11-50% in the 2080s. Without snowmaking the season would decline substantially by 37 – 57% in the 2050s.

Concurrent with the projected ski season losses, the estimated amount of snowmaking required increased by 36-144% in the scenarios for the 2020s. Required snowmaking amounts increased by 48-187% in the scenarios for the 2050s. The ability of individual ski areas to absorb additional snowmaking costs may be the crucial factor in remaining economically viable.

ADAPTATIONS OF TOURISM REPRESENTATIVES

The tourism representatives at a political, entrepreneurial, operational and organisational level are not sitting back idly contemplating the consequences of a climate change. They are adapting right now in the expectation of climate change. The experiences with snow-deficient winters have shown them that the climate does not determine their economic activities, but, instead, constitutes a key resource and framework condition. The results of a focus group study among tourism representatives in Switzerland can be summed up as follows.

Climate change has been recognised as a problem for winter tourism. Those responsible for tourism know that what they can offer is highly dependent on snow and that they are at risk from snow-deficient winters. They are familiar with the potential consequences of climate change for winter tourism. While achieving snow-reliability constitutes a central topic, potential climatic change is seen as being only of relatively minor importance.

Climate change is not regarded as a catastrophe for winter tourism. The tourism representatives think that climatic change is presented in a highly exaggerated form by the media and also in science and politics. Although climate change could intensify the problems that already exist in ski areas at lower altitudes and speed up structural changes in the sector, the majority of ski resorts at medium and high altitudes, however, would scarcely be affected.

Climate change is already affecting the strategies and plans of the winter sport resorts today. The discussions held in the focus groups clearly revealed an ambivalent relationship to climate change. On the one hand, the representatives strongly distrust the information disseminated about climate change and play down its potential consequences, but on the other hand, they use climate change to legitimate forward strategies. Climate change and global warming, together with international competition, have been used as the key arguments for constructing artificial snowmaking facilities, as well as for extending existing ski runs and opening new ones in high-alpine regions (at above 3000 m).

The tourism representatives all agree that winter sports can only survive in the Alps if snow-reliability is guaranteed. Precisely, the smaller ski fields at lower altitudes either have their hands bound or can scarcely finance the necessary investments (e.g. snow cannons, levelling out ski slopes, opening higher-altitude chambers in skiing areas).

On the one hand, they do not have financial resources of their own, and on the other hand, banks are (now) only prepared to grant very restrictive loans to ski resorts at altitudes below 1500 m, which are not particularly profitable. Nevertheless, the representatives believe that smaller ski fields in the Alpine foothills play a key role in promoting the importance of skiing.

Opinions frequently differ a great deal, however, on whether non-profitable ski regions of this type should be retained and how their financing can be guaranteed. While a number of people are in favour of dismantling non-profitable cable-way and ski-lift operations and regard a certain 'healthy shrinkage' of the sector as necessary, others believe that there is an obligation to retain these ski fields for regional economic reasons. This is also increasing pressure for cableway companies to receive subsidies.

STRATEGIES

Climate change represents a new challenge for tourism, and particularly for winter tourism in mountain areas. It is not, however, the case that tourism's initial position will undergo a sudden, radical change.

Instead, climate change has to be viewed as a catalyst that will reinforce and accelerate the pace of structural change in the tourist industry and more clearly highlight the risks and opportunities inherent in tourist developments even now.

The emergence of a 2-tier society in the winter tourism sector – a few resorts and cableway-companies at a high profit and most resorts and companies unprofitable - will not be due to climate change alone, but to the general change in a competitive market as well. On the one hand, we have the top resorts with their already varied and attractive offers and high snow-reliability and, on the other hand, we have the smaller locations with their less-extensive developments, less-refined offers and restricted opportunities for further development.

Since climate change is a relatively long-term development in comparison to other trends in tourism, tourism managers and tourists will have every opportunity to adjust to the different constraints and adopt the corresponding strategies and measures (fig. 1). One of the most familiar measures in the struggle against snow-deficient winters is the construction of high cost artificial snowmaking facilities.

Figure 1: Adaptation strategies

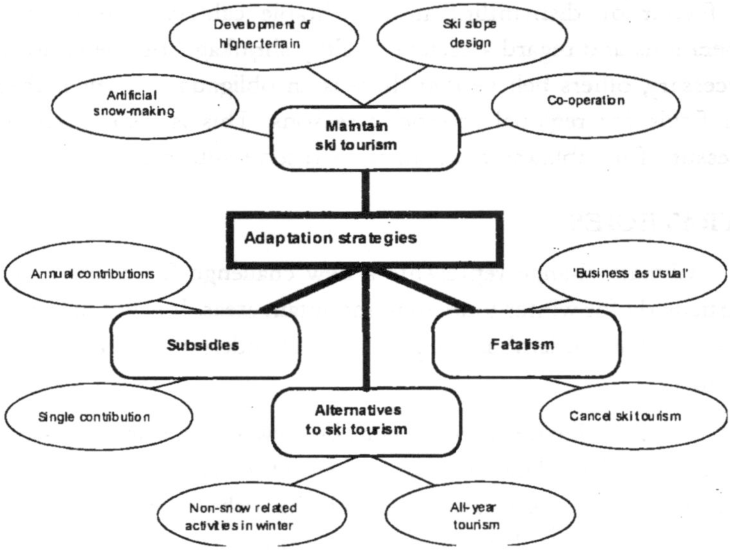

Adopting a fatalistic attitude towards climate change and its impacts should not be considered as a true strategy in this respect. Such attitudes are manifested by the fact that neither suppliers nor consumers alter their behaviour. This could also be described by using the term 'business as usual'. Another approach that can be classified under the heading of 'fatalism' is when tourist transport facilities that were used for winter sports are closed down and dismantled without any attempt at promoting and reinforcing other types of tourism – in other words, when withdrawal from ski tourism is not actively planned.

A fatalistic attitude of this type is most readily evident amongst the operators of small, isolated ski-lifts at lower altitudes who experienced severe financial difficulties as a result of the snow-deficient winters.

CONCLUSIONS

Global warming is a challenge for the tourism industry in mountain areas. But warmer temperatures and a longer summer season are of minor importance. Over all, climate change is a threat for mountain tourism due to less snow, less glaciers, but more extreme events (e.g. landslides).

Winter tourism depends on good snow conditions and is highly sensitive to snow-deficient winters. Climate research findings show that there will be an increase in the number of winters with little snow on account of climate change.

The tourism representatives will not just sit back idly in the face of climate change. They are reacting to the deteriorating snow conditions and the changes in demand. Technical measures, especially artificial snowmaking, to maintain ski tourism rank at the forefront. Tourists demand good snow conditions, and hence, this is what has to be offered by the ski resorts.

In any case, the impacts of climate change will involve significant costs for tourism. One of the most important questions will be, how young people would start skiing/snowboarding, if there is only little snow in the big towns and if the little and cheap ski lifts for families at small distances to these towns will be dismantled due to climate change. Although indoor skiing is a growing industry in European towns, it is uncertain that indoor ski domes can replace the role of little ski resorts for beginners in the foothills.

As a sector of the economy that is severely affected by climate change, however, tourism needs to focus more on mitigation strategies in its own best interests. This holds particularly true for the traffic generated by national and international tourism and, above all, for air traffic. Tourist development and tourist projects not only need to be verified and evaluated in terms of their social and environmental compatibility but must also be assessed from the climate-compatibility angle.

6

Sports for Development and Peace

This report analyses in detail the potential contribution that sport can make towards achieving the United Nations Millennium Development Goals (MDGs). It provides an overview of the growing role that sports activities are playing in many United Nations programmes and crystallizes the lessons learned.

It also includes recommendations aimed at maximizing and mainstreaming the use of sport. United Nations efforts to assist countries to achieve the MDGs include various actors working in partnership for sustainable development and peace. In particular, the eighth MDG calls for concerted action to cultivate "a global partnership for development". This is an essential step towards realizing the objectives of the United Nations, and it can only be achieved if civil society, as well as Governments and international agencies, is fully engaged.

The world of sport presents a natural partnership for the United Nations system. By its very nature sport is about participation. It is about inclusion and citizenship. Sport brings individuals and communities together, highlighting commonalties and bridging cultural or ethnic divides.

Sport provides a forum to learn skills such as discipline, confidence and leadership and it teaches core principles such as tolerance, cooperation and respect. Sport teaches the value of effort and how to manage victory, as well as defeat. When these positive aspects of sport are emphasized, sport becomes a powerful vehicle through which the United Nations can work towards achieving its goals. This report views sport in a broad sense.

Incorporated into the definition of "sport" are all forms of physical activity that contribute to physical fitness, mental well-being and social interaction. These include play; recreation; organized, casual or competitive sport; and indigenous sports or games. The fundamental elements of sport make it a viable and practical tool to support the achievement of the MDGs.

Sport has an impact on health and reduces the likelihood of many diseases. Sports programmes serve as an effective tool for social mobilization, supporting health activities such as HIV/AIDS education and immunization campaigns. Sport can be a significant economic force, providing employment and contributing to local development. It is also a key site and natural draw for volunteer involvement. Furthermore, participation in sport supports the preservation of a clean and healthy environment.

The practice of sport is vital to the holistic development of young people, fostering their physical and emotional health and building valuable social connections.

It offers opportunities for play and selfexpression, beneficial especially for those young people with few other opportunities in their lives. Sport also provides healthy alternatives to harmful actions, such as drug abuse and involvement in crime. Within schools, physical education is an essential component of quality education. Not only do physical education programmes promote physical activity; there is evidence that such programmes correlate to improved academic performance.

Sport can cut across barriers that divide societies, making it a powerful tool to support conflict prevention and peace-building efforts, both symbolically on the global level and very practically within communities. When applied effectively, sports programmes promote social integration and foster tolerance, helping to reduce tension and generate dialogue. The convening power of sport makes it additionally compelling as a tool for advocacy and communications. The chief finding of the on Sport for Development and Peace is that well-designed sport-based initiatives are practical and cost-effective tools to achieve objectives in development and peace. Sport is a powerful vehicle that should be increasingly considered by the United Nations as complementary to existing activities.

The Task Force therefore strongly recommends that:

1. Sport should be better integrated into the development agenda.
2. Sport should be incorporated as a useful tool in programmes for development and peace.
3. Sport-based initiatives should be included in the country programmes of United Nations agencies, where appropriate and according to locally assessed needs.
4. Programmes promoting sport for development and peace need greater attention and resources by Governments and the United Nations system.
5. Communications-based activities using sport should focus on well-targeted advocacy and social mobilization, particularly at the national and local levels.
6. A final recommendation of the Task Force is that the most effective way to implement programmes that use sport for development and peace is through partnerships.

INTRODUCTION

In July 2002, the Secretary-General of the United Nations convened an Inter-Agency Task Force to review activities involving sport within the United Nations system. The aim of the Task Force was to promote the more systematic and coherent use of sport in development and peace activities, particularly at the community level, and to generate greater support for such activities among Governments and sport-related organizations. The Task Force was also asked to establish an inventory of existing sport-for-development programmes,1 identify instructive examples and encourage the United Nations system to incorporate sport into its activities and work towards achieving the Millennium Development Goals (MDGs).

With these aims in mind, the on Sport for Development and Peace was formed, bringing together agencies with significant experience using sport in their work, including ILO, UNESCO, WHO, UNDP, UNV, UNEP, UNHCR, UNICEF, UNODC and UNAIDS. The Task Force was co-chaired by Mr. Adolf Ogi, the Special Adviser to the Secretary-General on Sport for Development and Peace, and Ms. Carol Bellamy, Executive Director of UNICEF. Secretariat support was provided by the non-governmental organization (NGO) Right To Play (formerly Olympic Aid).

Members of the Task Force were designated by the heads of the participating United Nations organizations. Between October 2002 and March 2003, the Task Force met twice: first, to determine its overall strategy and, second, to decide upon recommendations.

Participating agencies prepared submissions based upon their experience using sport and its relevance to their work. A smaller Drafting Committee met a further three times to determine the structure and content of the report. The submissions were then consolidated and a report was prepared by the Secretariat and Co-Chairs, in close consultation with participants.

The Task Force sought to crystallize the lessons learned from the growing experience within the United Nations system of using sport as a tool for development and peace, as well as to seize the growing interest in the world of sport in United Nations activities. Several concrete steps have been taken in recent years in support of the use of sport for development and peace. These include recommendations emanating from MINEPS III, the UNESCO meeting of ministers for physical education and sport in 1999; the World Health Assembly resolution WHA55.23 in 2002 concerning the WHO Global Strategy on Diet, Physical Activity and Health; the decision by UNEP's Governing Council in 2003 to initiate a long-term strategy on sport and the environment; and a UNICEF Executive Directive in early 2003 encouraging all field offices to consider sport in their programming. Similarly, in the sports world, various sports federations and organizations have demonstrated an increasing awareness about the broader potential of sport.

However, much more should be done. Sport has yet to be mainstreamed into the development agenda or the United Nations system. In general, sports initiatives to date have been ad hoc, informal and isolated. The time is ripe to develop a coherent and systematic strategy for increasing the use of sport within the United Nations. A common framework needs to be established that draws together sport-related initiatives and actors across the different sectors.

REALIZING THE POTENTIAL OF SPORT AS A TOOL FOR DEVELOPMENT AND PEACE

Sport is far more than a luxury or a form of entertainment. Access to and participation in sport is a human right and essential for individuals of all ages to lead healthy and fulfilling lives. Sport—from play and physical activity to organized competitive sport—has an important role in all societies.

Sport is critical to a child's development. It teaches core values such as cooperation and respect. It improves health and reduces the likelihood of disease. It is a significant economic force providing employment and contributing to local development. And it brings individuals and communities together, bridging cultural or ethnic divides. Sport offers a cost-effective tool to meet many development and peace challenges, and help achieve the MDGs.

The potential of sport as a tool for development and peace has yet to be fully realized. The use of sport remains outside the mainstream of thinking among United Nations agencies. While sport and play are repeatedly acknowledged as a human right, they are not always seen as a priority and have even been called the "forgotten right".2 Sport is seen as a by-product of development, not as an engine. This report shows why sport must play a stronger role in the development agenda. By demonstrating the contribution sport can make when it is used in a coordinated and strategic way, the report challenges the United Nations and its partners to integrate sport into their work. In addition, it aims to garner new support for such initiatives among sport-related organizations, Governments and the private sector, suggesting ways to move forward in partnership with civil society.

THE SCOPE OF SPORT

This report views sport in a broad sense. Incorporated into the definition of "sport" are all forms of physical activity that contribute to physical fitness, mental well-being and social interaction. These include play; recreation; organized, casual or competitive sport; and indigenous sports or games.

Play, especially among children, is any physical activity that is fun and participatory. It is often unstructured and free from adult direction. Recreation is more organized than play and generally entails physically active leisure activities. Sport is more organized again and involves rules or customs and sometimes competition. Importantly, play, physical recreation and sport are all freely chosen activities undertaken for pleasure.

The concept of "sport for all" is central to this understanding of sport. "Sport for all" initiatives aim to maximize access to and participation in appropriate forms of physical activity. Emphasis is placed on participation and the inclusion of all groups in society, regardless of gender, age, ability or race.

Given the Task Force's emphasis on "sport for all", elite competitive sport generally lies outside the scope of this report, although at times references are made to it.4 The aim of United Nations activities involving sport is not the creation of new sporting champions and the development of sport but rather the use of sport in broader development and peace-building activities. While in some instances such activities may lead to the development of sport, the primary desired outcome is to contribute to overall development via sport-related projects.

MAXIMIZING THE POSITIVE ASPECTS OF SPORT

Many of the core values inherent in sport are compatible with the principles necessary for development and peace, such as fair play, cooperation, sharing and respect. The life skills learned through sport help empower individuals and enhance psychosocial well-being, such as increased resiliency, selfesteem and connections with others.

These features of sport are beneficial to people of all ages, but they are especially vital to the healthy development of young people. Sport, however, is a reflection of society. It should be acknowledged that sport, like many aspects of society, simultaneously encompasses some of the worst human traits, including violence, corruption, discrimination, hooliganism, excessive nationalism, cheating and drug abuse. However, these negative aspects of sport by no means outweigh its potential positive benefits. The United Nations has the ability to help Governments and communities harness the positive aspects of sport and channel them in a coordinated way towards the pursuit of the MDGs.

SPORT AND SUSTAINABLE HUMAN DEVELOPMENT

Central to the United Nations notion of development is sustainable human development, which recognizes that development is more than economic growth. Development is a process of enlarging people's choices and increasing the opportunities available to all members of society. Based on the principles of inclusion, equity and sustainability, emphasis is on the importance of increasing opportunities for the current generation as well as generations to come. The basic human capabilities that are necessary for this are to "lead long and healthy lives, to be knowledgeable, to have access to the resources needed for a decent standard of living and to be able to participate in the life of the community". Sport can directly help build these capabilities.

Participation in sport has significant physical benefits, contributing to people's ability to lead long and healthy lives, improving well-being, extending life expectancy and reducing the likelihood of several major non-communicable diseases, particularly heart disease, diabetes and certain cancers. Sport also provides psychosocial benefits, such as fostering social integration and teaching coping mechanisms, as well as psychological benefits, such as reducing depression and improving concentration. Sport further builds human capabilities by increasing knowledge and contributing to education. Incorporating physical education into the school curriculum and providing opportunities for recreation improve a child's ability to learn, with evidence indicating that it also increases attendance and overall achievement.

Sport also educates people about the body, raising awareness and respect for their bodies and those of others, critical for healthy living and the prevention of diseases, like HIV/AIDS. Similarly, participation in outdoor sports raises awareness and respect for the environment, teaching people about the importance of a clean and healthy environment. Sport is also a key component of social life, directly engaging communities. It brings people together in a fun and participatory way. It helps create social relationships, build connections and improve communication between individuals and groups. Sport also mobilizes volunteers and promotes active community involvement, helping to build social capital and strengthen the social fabric.

SPORT AND ECONOMIC DEVELOPMENT

While sport is essential to human development, it also contributes to economic development. The economic potential of sport is highlighted by its economic weight, resulting from activities such as the manufacture of sporting goods, sports events, sport-related services and the media. In the UK, for example, the value added of sports activities is estimated to be 1.7 per cent of GDP, with sport-related turnover comparable to that of the automotive and food industries.

Beyond being an economic force in itself, sport is also a potential catalyst for economic development. A physically active population is a healthier population, improving the productivity of the workforce and increasing economic output. Sport and physical activity also provide one of the most costeffective forms of preventive medicine, with the potential to cut health-care costs dramatically. Sport adds further to economic development by providing a cheap method of improving employability, especially among young people. By teaching core skills essential for the workplace such as teamwork, leadership, discipline and the value of effort, it provides young people with a constructive activity that helps reduce levels of juvenile crime and antisocial behaviour and, in instances of child labour, provides a meaningful substitute for work.

Sport can also be an engine for local economic development and job creation. Sports programmes provide employment opportunities as well as stimulate demand for goods and services. Sport is also an important source of public and private expenditure, such as that spent on infrastructure, during major events and on consumption. Together, these factors result in sport having considerable potential for initiating economic development.

SPORT AND PEACE

The potential links between sport and peace are also powerful. From international events to the grass roots, sport brings people together in a way that can cross boundaries and break down barriers, making the playing field a simple and often apolitical site for initiating contact between antagonistic groups. Consequently, sport can be an ideal forum for resuming social dialogue and bridging divides, highlighting the similarities between people and breaking down prejudice.7 The popularity of sport and its convening power further contribute to sport being a powerful voice for communicating messages of peace and a site for symbolic public acts on the global and local levels. Sport is an effective element in community-based initiatives that aim to create sustainable peace.

The skills and values learned through sport are many of the same skills and values taught in peace education to resolve and prevent conflict and create conditions conducive to peace, from the interpersonal to the international.8 Well-crafted sports activities teach respect, honesty, communication, cooperation, empathy, and how and why to adhere to rules. Sport is a powerful way to communicate these values, especially to young people, in a way that is fun and participatory. For refugees, displaced persons, orphans and former child soldiers, sport offers a sense of normality providing structure in destabilizing environments, and serves as a means to channel energies positively.

SPORT AS A HUMAN RIGHT

Sport is more than a practical method to achieve development and peace. The opportunity to participate in and enjoy sport and play is a human right that must be promoted and supported. Sport and play are therefore not only a means, but also an end. While the Office of the High Commissioner for Human Rights (OHCHR) was not represented on the Task Force, there was nonetheless consensus about the importance of examining the right to sport and play, especially given its prominence in several key instruments used by the agencies involved.9 That sport is a human right is explicitly embodied in article 1 of the Charter of Physical Education and Sport adopted by UNESCO in 1978. The charter states: "The practice of physical education and sport is a fundamental human right for all." It stresses that every person is entitled to participate in sport, including especially women, young people, the elderly and the disabled.

Similarly, a child's right to play is enshrined in article 31 of the Convention on the Rights of the Child, which recognizes "the right of the child to rest and leisure, to engage in play and recreational activities appropriate to the age of the child". This article continues, stating that not only do children have the right to play; they also have the right to the provision of the opportunity to play, requiring States to "encourage the provision of appropriate and equal opportunities for cultural, artistic, recreational and leisure activity". Several other United Nations instruments also acknowledge the importance of access to and participation in sport, such as the Convention on the Elimination of All Forms of Discrimination against Women. Similarly, ILO Conventions Nos. 138 and 182 concerning child labour require Governments to establish policies for the rehabilitation of child labourers. Here, sport is considered an effective policy tool. In spite of these international instruments, the right to sport and play is often denied. In many cases this is because of discrimination, particularly by gender and ability. It is also frequently due to political neglect of the importance of sport in society, exemplified by the decline in spending on physical education and the lack of appropriate spaces and resources necessary for sport.

However, the fact that access to and participation in sport and play are human rights creates the responsibility to ensure that these rights are upheld. It places a duty on Governments, the United Nations system and others to ensure that the opportunity for participation in sport and play exists, allowing all people to enjoy their right to sport and play. OHCHR may wish to look further into these issues and the potential of sport to promote respect for human rights.

SPORT IN PURSUIT OF THE MILLENNIUM DEVELOPMENT GOALS

Sport directly contributes to the pursuit of the Millennium Development Goals. It is an innovative and effective tool to assist existing efforts to achieve specific targets such as those concerning education, gender equality, HIV/AIDS and the reduction of major diseases. More broadly, well-designed sports programmes are also a cost-effective way to contribute significantly to health, education, development and peace and a powerful medium through which to mobilize societies as well as communicate key messages.

As one of the richest and most developed aspects of civil society, and as a powerful international network of private sector actors and organizations, sport opens new avenues for creative partnerships through which to achieve the Untied Nations development goals.

SPORT AND HEALTH

Sport and physical activity are essential for improving health and well-being, an aim integral to the achievement of the MDGs. Appropriate forms of sport and physical activity can play a significant role to prevent as well as help cure many of the world's leading non-communicable diseases.

Evidence shows that regular participation in physical activity programmes provides all people with a wide range of physical, social and mental health benefits. Such active participation also complements strategies to improve diet, discourage the use of tobacco, alcohol and drugs and enhance functional capacity. Consequently, physical activity is an effective method of disease prevention for the individual and, for nations, a cost-effective way to improve public health.

THE GLOBAL RISE IN NON-COMMUNICABLE DISEASES

The health burden from preventable non-communicable diseases, such as cardiovascular diseases, cancer, diabetes and chronic respiratory diseases, is increasing significantly throughout the world. WHO estimates that mortality, morbidity and disability resulting from these leading diseases currently account for approximately 60 per cent of all deaths and 43 per cent of the global disease burden.11 These rates are expected to rise to 73 per cent and 60 per cent respectively by 2020.

THE RISE IN PHYSICAL INACTIVITY

Unhealthy diets, tobacco use and physical inactivity are the dominant factors causing the chronic diseases listed above and are now leading public-health issues in most countries. Of the disease-causing factors, physical inactivity is estimated to directly cause 1.9 million deaths globally, while also indirectly contributing to diseases and deaths resulting from factors including high blood pressure, high cholesterol and obesity (see figure 1 on the following page). Globally, over 60 per cent of adults do not participate in a sufficient amount of sport and physical activity, largely due to changes in lifestyle such as inactivity at work, sedentary forms of recreation, like television and computers, and excessive use of "passive" modes of transport.

Such a sedentary lifestyle also contributes to obesity. Those most likely to be physically inactive are women, older people, the disabled and people from lower socio-economic groups. In addition, while physical activity is critical for the holistic development of young people, one third of adolescents are insufficiently active, with girls offered fewer opportunities to be active than boys. This is especially problematic given that patterns of physical activity set when young usually form the basis for lifelong activity.

THE HEALTH BENEFITS OF SPORT AND PHYSICAL ACTIVITY

Engaging in sport has multiple health benefits. Physical activity can reduce the risk both of dying prematurely from non-communicable diseases and of developing illnesses ranging from cardiovascular diseases, cancer and diabetes to stress, anxiety and depression. It also helps prevent and reduce hypertension, control body weight, prevent and control osteoporosis and manage chronic pain. While it is critical that everyone regularly participates in sport and physical activity, regardless of age, ability, gender or background, physical activity provides additional benefits to certain groups, for example:

- Among young people, physical activity contributes to healthy bones, efficient heart and lung function and improved motor skills and cognitive function.
- Among women, physical activity helps prevent hip fractures and reduce the effects of osteoporosis.
- Among older people, physical activity enhances functional capacity, helping maintain quality of life and independence.

THE ECONOMIC BENEFITS OF SPORT FOR HEALTH

Medical evidence shows that participation in physical activity, as part of an overall healthy lifestyle, is the most cost-effective and sustainable way to tackle the rise in non-communicable diseases. Improving public health through increasing opportunities to participate in sport offers large economic benefits—particularly in developing countries where health resources are already stretched, making prevention especially essential.

Beyond improving public health and reducing health-care costs, sport and physical activity also provide significant economic benefits through increased productivity.

For example, in the United States of America, where physical inactivity added US$ 75 billion to medical costs in 2000, it is estimated that one dollar (US$ 1) spent on physical activity results in a three dollar and twenty cent (US$ 3.20) saving in medical costs.13 In Canada, it is estimated that physical activity increases productivity by the equivalent of Can$ 513 per worker per year, resulting from reduced absenteeism, turnover and injury as well as an increase in productivity.14 Consequently, sport results in not only positive benefits for individuals, but also significant economic benefits for businesses, communities and nations.

To highlight the importance of sport and physical activity for health, WHO dedicated World Health Day 2002 to "Move for Health"15 and World No Tobacco Day 2002 to "Tobacco-Free

Sports: Play It Clean". In 2003, WHO further expanded the "Move for Health" initiative with the aim of promoting sustained participation in physical activity and "sport for all" in all member States as part of an integrated approach to the prevention of non-communicable diseases, health promotion and socio-economic development.

This initiative urges member States to celebrate a "Move for Health" day each year, promote physical activity as essential for health and well-being and develop partnership-based global and national strategies on diet, physical activity and health. The recommended levels of physical activity

KEY CONSIDERATIONS REGARDING SPORT AND HEALTH

The correlation between an increase in disease and a decrease in physical activity requires that sport become a priority in policies by Governments and concerned stakeholders at all levels and in all sectors. The economic benefits of a physically active population include improved public health, reduced health-care costs and increased productivity, further highlighting the importance of sport and physical activity as a priority for Governments and concerned stakeholders.

Care should be given to ensure that "sport for all" and physical activity programmes are appropriately designed and culturally relevant. They should also be inclusive of those groups that receive additional health benefits from physical activity while lacking equal opportunity to participate, especially women, persons with disabilities, young people and older people.

The global "Move for Health" day/initiative should serve as a partnership-based opportunity for developing and/or strengthening global, national and local policies and programmes on physical activity within an integrated framework of non-communicable disease prevention, health and development.

SPORT AND EDUCATION

Education is central to the achievement of all of the MDGs, and sport has a natural place in education, whether the approach used is formal, non-formal or informal. In schools, physical education is a key component of a quality education and can be used to promote schooling among young people. Outside the classroom, sport is a "school for life", teaching basic values and life skills important for holistic development. Sport is also a powerful vehicle for public education, while sporting events can effectively increase awareness and galvanize support and action around key issues see "Sport and Communication").

SPORT AS A "SCHOOL FOR LIFE"

Sport is an ideal school for life. The skills learned through play, physical education and sport are fundamental to the holistic development of young people. These skills, such as cooperation and confidence, are essential for social cohesion and are carried throughout adult life. Sport actively educates young people about the importance of certain key values, such as honesty, fair play, respect for self and others, and adherence to the rules and respect for their importance. It provides a forum for them to learn how to cope with competition, not only how to lose but also how to win.

Sport is a way to build understanding for the value of common bonds. And traditional games, those native to an area or culture, can be especially effective in this regard. For example, some benefits of encouraging traditional games are that they emphasize the importance of diversity, contribute to inclusion and help people understand their own identity and those of others. Traditional sports and games are also usually lower in cost in terms of facilities and equipment than common sports.

Since 2000, Youth Education through Sport (YES), a sport and education programme led by youth for youth, has reached 25,000 young people in Zimbabwe's 10 provinces. Each participant must make a commitment to stay in school and to volunteer in the community. The aim of the programme is for young people to adopt life skills, become peer educators and contribute to their communities as positive role models.

SPORT, EDUCATION AND INCLUSION

It is imperative that sports programmes both in and out of school include all people and ensure equal opportunity to participate regardless of gender, ethnicity or ability. Girls, education and sport: The skills and values learned through sport are especially important for girls, given that they have fewer opportunities than boys for social interaction outside the home and beyond family networks. Ensuring that girls receive equitable access to quality education is central to development. Since achieving education for all and reaching girls who are denied access to basic education means expanding the way education is provided, non-formal forms of provision such as sportrelated programmes should be considered.

In Romania, UNICEF's education programme is using sport to increase school participation among the Roma community. The project aims to motivate children to attend school regularly as well as improve the gender balance in education by providing an opportunity for girls and boys to participate in sports teams, conditional upon school attendance and academic performance.

Through sport, girls are given the chance to be leaders and improve their confidence and selfesteem. As girls begin to participate in sport, they also acquire new interpersonal links and access to new opportunities, allowing them to become more engaged in school and community life. Sport provides young people with their own space, both physically and emotionally, which is especially important for girls. Sports teams and leagues often provide girls a forum to develop a sense of camaraderie and share time and values with other girls.

Providing girls with access to sport can also contribute to achieving gender parity in education. Given that sport is a traditionally male domain, girls' participation in sport challenges stereotypes of girls and women, breaking down entrenched attitudes. And, as female athletes gain recognition, they become mentors for others.

Physical education and the disabled: Giving young people with disabilities the opportunity to participate in physical education programmes at school and through community clubs is crucial given the additional benefits they receive from sport and physical activity. Sport, education and refugees: Education is voluntary for most refugees given that they are not citizens in their host countries. Sports programmes in refugee schools provide an additional incentive to get young people to school. Anecdotal evidence from UNHCR shows that including physical education and team sports programmes in refugee schools attracts new groups of students to school, often girls, that otherwise do not attend. Sports programmes increase attendance rates and reduce antisocial and uncooperative behaviour, including violence.

Since 1997, IOC and UNHCR have been working in Bhutanese refugee camps in Nepal to offer structured sport and recreational activities for refugees. By providing the opportunity to play, the programme aims to improve the education in the camps, while also helping to heal the psychological effects of war and flight. UNHCR is working closely with many partners to provide refugees with sports activities in refugee communities around the world. In Peshawar, UNHCR partners with the NGO Right To Play and Insan Foundation Pakistan to provide sports and physical education programmes to Afghan refugees. The programmes contribute to the rise in school attendance rates, especially among girls, and, according to parents and teachers, reduce aggression and violence.

SPORT, EDUCATION AND PHYSICAL EDUCATION

Physical education is an essential component of quality education and an integral part of lifelong learning. The neglect of physical education reduces the quality of education, with negative future impacts on public health and health budgets. Physical education is the only subject in the curriculum that focuses specifically on the body. In doing so, it helps teach young people respect for the body—their own as well as others—and helps them respond to many of the challenges faced by young people, including the threat of HIV/AIDS and other sexually transmitted diseases, and the dangers of tobacco and drugs. Providing students with the opportunity to play sport at school ensures that they receive a well-rounded education that addresses body, mind and spirit.

Physical education is an effective means of promoting physical activity among young people. Given that rates of physical activity tend to decrease from adolescence, it is imperative that young people gain an appreciation of sport at school in order to ensure lifelong active and healthy living. In Mongolia, a UNESCO project funded by the Danish aid agency promotes sport at several learning centres throughout the country and supports physical education and sports events as part of the education curriculum.

Inside the classroom, there is strong evidence highlighting the positive correlations between participation in sport and academic achievement. One study found that children between the ages of 6 and 12 who do at least five hours per week of physical activity achieve better marks than those who are active for less than one hour.17 More generally, research shows that increasing the time spent on physical education in schools does not reduce marks in intellectual subjects but rather improves the ability of some students to learn and retain information.

Despite recognition of the positive impact sport has on education and child development, physical education is being increasingly marginalized in the education system. This includes a decrease in the amount of time allocated to physical education, the number of specially trained staff, the amount of training for physical education teachers and spending on resources needed to participate in sport, physical activity and games in school. Research conducted in 126 countries shows that the marginalization of physical education is near universal.18 The primary reason for this marginalization is that physical education is often seen as non-productive and non-intellectual and, hence, an inessential component of education, despite being a legal requisite in over 100 of the countries surveyed.

In January 2003, UNESCO hosted representatives from 103 countries at a Ministerial Round Table. One of the three key topics addressed was the importance of reversing the marginalization of physical education, given its effectiveness as a tool for health and physical development as well as for acquiring values necessary for social cohesion and intercultural dialogue. Physical education is an excellent means to put into practice many of the skills that are considered necessary outcomes of a modern education system, especially teamwork, cooperation, problem-solving and confidence-building. These are aspects of learning that involve knowledge, but knowledge alone is not sufficient; physical education provides a very practical way to imbue these skills.

KEY CONSIDERATIONS REGARDING SPORT AND EDUCATION

Sport provides an ideal "school for life", especially when activities are explicitly designed to teach key skills and values and ensure the empowerment of marginalized groups. Due to the negative future impact on public health and health budgets resulting from the neglect of physical education, Governments should acknowledge the importance of physical education and show their support by improving the provision of resources and staff training and allocating appropriate amounts of school time to physical education.

To achieve broader goals in education and development, sports programmes must focus on the development of the individual and not only on the development of technical sports skills. Sport and Sustainable Development Effective development must be sustainable and human-centred. Sustainable development requires that the needs of the present generation are met without compromising the ability of future generations to meet their own needs,19 and human development requires that people's choices are enlarged, providing all members of society with increased opportunities and the conditions necessary to live long and fulfilling lives.20 Well-designed sports programmes work to assist meeting the objectives of sustainable human development, by contributing to economic and social development and environmental sustainability.

SPORT AND ECONOMIC DEVELOPMENT

Sport is a catalyst for economic development. Globally, the sports sector is valued at US$ 36 billion and is predicted to expand by 3 to 5 per cent per year.21 Included in the sports sector are the manufacture of sporting goods, sport-related services, infrastructure development and sports events, including supplementary effects from spectators, sponsors, vendors and the media. These elements of the sports economy are interconnected, both contributing to and benefiting from the development of sport. Sport can be an effective stimulus for economic development, especially at the local level. The linkages between the different elements of the sports sector are highly effective when harnessed locally because of existing economies of scale. Individually, each of the various sectors of the sports economy can create activity, jobs and wealth. When several are combined together into a single strategy, it is possible to achieve additional economic gains because of the synergies that result. The local economic potential of sport is further enhanced when supported by national "sport for all" strategies.

By encouraging sport and sport-based economic activities, it is possible to initiate a "virtuous circle" in which new forms of activity are generated, requiring additional goods and services, creating jobs and contributing to economic development.22 Here, the provision of financial and technical assistance, such as coach training or assistance with technical aspects of sporting goods manufacturing, are highly beneficial and provide the support to initiate such a cycle. Both the design and implementation of sport-based local economic development strategies must be participatory, encouraging and facilitating partnerships between local stakeholders, including

Governments, UN agencies, NGOs, community groups, employers and employees.

Such strategies should take an integrated approach, considering activities that concern small and medium-sized enterprises (SMEs), employment creation and training, and the development of infrastructure. Manufacture of sporting goods: There is high consumer demand for sporting goods. However, many of these goods are prohibitively expensive in the developing context. This unfilled demand provides opportunities for local SMEs to use existing skills and facilities to produce specialized sporting equipment at a price that is locally affordable.23 Sport and job creation: Sport is an effective tool for job creation.24 By developing new activities based on sport or by more effectively using existing sports facilities, sports- and community-based programmes can create jobs, particularly for young people, and especially where unmet demand is identified.

In Jonava, Lithuania, UN-Habitat assisted in the creation of recreational zones to provide areas for all people to use free of charge, addressing equality and social inclusion. The development of these zones increased employment opportunities for the unemployed and included vocational training and work experience in the environment field, teaching skills increasingly in demand in the region.

Sport and employment training: Sport-related initiatives can improve the capacity of the labour force. Beyond the increased productivity generated by having a physically active workforce, sport is a valuable employment training tool. Sport teaches skills such as the value of effort and how to work as a team, thus improving employability. This is especially effective when focused on young people and marginalized groups.

In Albania, the Government, the NGO Unione Italiana Sport per Tutti and ILO are providing sport as a means to help young people cope with the negative side effects of the transition to a market economy, including youth unemployment of up to 25 per cent, drugs and poverty. Through a network of youth centres, young people are given their own space and an opportunity to socialize and to participate in sport and recreational activities, while also receiving advice, counselling and assistance with jobseeking.

Sports infrastructure: Economic development can be stimulated by the construction or rehabilitation of sports infrastructure, whether large facilities or small projects, such as levelling a space to make it safe and suitable for playing.

Therefore, open spaces and the development of sports infrastructure are important in urban planning. The economic benefits of developing infrastructure include employment and investment during construction, as well as ongoing employment to manage the facility and the activities within it.

Once constructed, some sports facilities can be used for multiple purposes, including by schools and community groups for cultural, social and other activities. In Mozambique, the Minister for Youth and Sports and local government are rehabilitating sports facilities with the support of IOC and other sports federations in Boane and Namaacha. In parallel, ILO, UNICEF and Right To Play are running coach-to-coach training programmes that focus on using sport as a community development and social mobilization tool, in particular concerning issues surrounding health, such as sports festivals held on World AIDS Day.

SPORT AND SOCIAL DEVELOPMENT

More than stimulating economic growth, effectively designed sports programmes strengthen basic human capabilities, create connections between individuals, and teach core values and life skills. They are a valuable tool to initiate social development and improve social cohesion, especially when implemented with young people. Together, the benefits from such programmes provide a powerful means to tackle social exclusion, rehabilitate child labourers and integrate marginalized groups into their communities.

In Zambia, Edusport Outreach International uses netball, basketball, athletics, aerobics, dance and volleyball programmes to train young people in coaching their peers and to teach life skills to over 10,000 street children, orphans and at-risk youth. The success of this programme has led to its being used as a model for programmes in Botswana, South Africa, Tanzania and Uganda. Drug abuse: When social and personal skills are combined, sport can be an effective medium to intervene in a person's decision to abuse or not abuse drugs.

While participation in sport does not inherently lead to a drug-free lifestyle, well-designed sports programmes, run by skilled and credible coordinators, help to reduce high-risk behaviours. This is especially true when the elements of sport are combined with the structured provision of drug-related information and life-skills training.25 In 2001, UNODC, the US National Basketball Association and a number of other partners cooperated in a high-profile camp for young teens from the former Yugoslavia. The camp focused on leadership building, conflict resolution and the importance of living a healthy lifestyle without drugs.

In Georgia, more than 46,000 children from 2,028 schools have participated in regional football tournaments sponsored by government agencies, UNICEF, businesses and NGOs.

The matches are designed to encourage a healthy lifestyle for young people, promoting the message that "smoking, drinking and taking drugs can't compare to the extraordinary high of kicking a winning goal". Crime: Factors that contribute to young people turning to crime include the absence of positive role models, a lack of self-discipline and boredom. Sport can tackle these causes of juvenile crime by helping disaffected youth make positive connections with adults and peers, by integrating them into constructive activities within society and by providing a useful activity for their time.

In the UK, a recent report showed that sports programmes in high-crime areas helped reduce juvenile crime, vandalism and delinquency and stopped many young people from reoffending. In Brazil, UNICEF supports a detention centre for young people in trouble with the law.

After academic classes, they play football, learn judo and practise gymnastics, helping them to channel frustrations and learn new ways to deal with anger. Gender equity: Sport can be an effective tool for empowering girls and women, given that they are often excluded from participating and enjoying the physical and psychosocial benefits offered by sport. By directly challenging and dispelling misperceptions about women's capabilities, integrated sports programmes help to reduce discrimination and widen the role prescribed to women. In the US, research shows that regular participation in sport correlates to girls being less sexually active, lower rates of teen pregnancy and higher academic performance.

In Zimbabwe, IDSP, a division of Commonwealth Games Canada, partners with provincial health units to deliver biweekly aerobics programmes, open to all women in urban and rural communities and reaching an estimated 200,000 participants.

Included are discussions on women's rights, parental guidance, basic health, family planning, pre- and post-natal care, HIV/AIDS education and counselling services. Persons with disabilities: Sport can integrate persons with disabilities into society, providing an arena for positive social interaction, reducing isolation and breaking down prejudice.

Sports programmes for the disabled are also a cost-effective method of rehabilitation. They are highly therapeutic, improving motor skills and increasing mobility, self-sufficiency and self-confidence. The Norwegian Confederation of Sport and Olympic Committee (NIF) supports sports programmes for the disabled. For example, in Zimbabwe it is working with the Zimbabwe Olympic Committee and Commonwealth Sport Development Programme (now IDSP) to assist people with disabilities, enabling them to participate in a sport of their choice.

UNVs, working with UNDP and ILO, combined karate with vocational training programmes for the physically disabled in Kenya, where over 1 million workers are disabled, in order to help improve motor skills and mobility as well as confidence. Child labour: As part of a quality education, sport can help to rehabilitate child labourers, strengthening their capacities, serving as part of a replacement activity to work and giving them the opportunity to play. Sport can also be used as a platform to mobilize young people within the community against child labour.

SPORT AND THE ENVIRONMENT

The relationship between sport and the environment includes both the impact of sport on the environment and the impact of the environment on sport. All sports activities, events and facilities have an impact on the environment, creating an "ecological footprint". Although sport is generally not a major cause of pollution, its cumulative impact is significant and can include pesticides, erosion, waste generation and habitat loss. As a result, the negative impact of sport on the environment should always be minimized.

UNEP is working with major sports organizations, including the Olympic Movement and the World Federation of the Sporting Goods Industry, to ensure that major sports events and sports goods are "green". It is also important for sport to be pursued in an environmentally sustainable manner, given that the deterioration of environmental conditions reduces the health, well-being and living standards of individuals and communities as well as their levels of physical activity.

Factors such as waterborne, airborne and soil-borne pollutants and ultraviolet radiation impact negatively on people's ability and willingness to participate in sport. Conversely, a cleaner environment encourages people to be more connected to the natural environment and to be more physically active. Participation in sport also requires the provision of appropriate, safe and clean places to play, whether specific facilities or parks and open spaces. Maximizing participation in sport therefore requires the creation of a clean, suitable and sustainable environment.

The football club MYSA, located in the slum of Mathare in Nairobi, allocates points to its teams on the basis of wins, losses, draws and garbage collection, coupling the health benefits from a clean environment with those from participation in sport. The inherent link between a clean environment and participation in sport is part of what makes sport a powerful tool for communicating environmental messages and encouraging action to clean up the environment.

SPORT AND VOLUNTEERISM

Volunteers are an important strategic resource for sports programmes that should be actively mobilized. Sport everywhere relies on volunteers, whether community-based matches or international events. For example, the Sydney 2000 Olympic Games deployed 47,000 volunteers. Once involved through sport, volunteers can then be mobilized to donate their time to other activities.

Given that sport is a key site for volunteer involvement, sport should be used to promote volunteerism, especially among youth whose participation is a strong predictor of volunteering in later life. Volunteerism provides benefits to the individual, such as self-fulfilment, skill acquisition, increased understanding and social integration. It also benefits society, through impacts including economic growth, social welfare, community participation, generation of trust and reciprocity, and the broadening of social interaction through new networks. Consequently, volunteerism creates social capital, helping to build and consolidate social cohesion and stability. Sport is a key way to encourage volunteerism within societies and achieve the resulting social benefits.

In the UK, the contribution made by volunteers to sport is estimated to be greater than government and lottery funding combined.33 Volunteers are a key resource in sport for development programmes, including UNVs, White Helmets (Argentina), VSOs (UK), Peace Corps (US) and volunteer coaches used by NGOs including SCORE and Right To Play. SCORE, an NGO based in South Africa, recruits international and local volunteers to implement sports programmes in schools and in underprivileged communities. Volunteers work on activities including physical education programmes, organized sports activities in and after school, sports festivals, sport for the disabled and the development of community sports clubs.

Key considerations regarding sport and development In order to maximize the economic potential of sport, development strategies should take an integrated, coherent approach, with emphasis placed on the value of stimulating growth at the local level. Sports programmes aimed at supporting social development must be well designed, led by trained personnel, focused on the development of the individual, and inclusive of all groups regardless of age, race, gender or ability.

Consideration must be given to the potential harm or adverse effects of sports activities on the environment. The positive environmental achievements of sports organizations and the organizers of sports events should be recognized, as this can inspire others to increase their efforts in support of a sustainable environment. Volunteers are a strategic resource that should be mobilized when implementing sport-for development programmes. Furthermore, sport is a key site and natural draw for volunteer involvement.

SPORT AND PEACE

Sport is an international language. Its ability to cross cultures enables sport-related programmes to bridge social and ethnic divides. As a result, sport can be a powerful tool to promote peace, both symbolically on the global level and very practically within communities. The power of sport can be used as a tool for preventing conflict as well as an element for building sustainable peace. When applied effectively, sports programmes promote social integration and foster tolerance. These core values are the same as those necessary for lasting peace. In post-conflict environments in particular, this can work to reduce tensions and generate dialogue.

COMMUNITY-BASED PEACE INITIATIVES

The use of sport to promote peace is extremely effective in programmes at the community level, since they directly involve those affected by conflict and social tension.

Sport is often denied in times of instability and yet it offers a sense of normality, especially for young people. Sports programmes provide structure in an unstructured and destabilizing environment and serve as a means to channel energies away from aggression or self-destruction. Concurrently, they help build the individual skills and values necessary to avoid conflict and to ensure peace. Various groups benefit particularly from sport for- peace programmes.

In Somalia, UNICEF and UNESCO are working towards promoting peace through sport with programmes that both train youth in peaceful conflict resolution skills while doing sports training and provide resources and encourage and support inter-district and regional sport-peace tournaments. The aim is to build the capacity of sport while creating a protective environment to help rehabilitate and reintegrate young people living in a post-conflict situation. Young people: In many circumstances young people lack hope, as well as the practical means to change their situation.

Sport is a medium to help build character and confidence, preparing young people to better meet the challenges of a competitive world. These elements can be especially beneficial in the care and support of orphans. *Sharek*, the Arabic word for participate, is a UNDP initiative for youth in the West Bank and Gaza. When designing and implementing their own programmes with the help of UNVs, young Palestinians overwhelmingly chose sport as a necessary element of their lives.

The Danish Cross Cultures Project Association and UEFA support 185 "Open Fun Football Schools" for 37,000 children between 8 and 14 years of age as part of a project to nurture peaceful coexistence in countries such as Bosnia and Herzegovina, the former Yugoslav Republic of Macedonia, and Serbia and Montenegro. Young people participate in football training camps that aim to engender team spirit and help bridge ethnic and religious divides.

Refugees and IDPs: The psychosocial benefits from the practice of sport help to address the trauma of flight and the distress resulting from displacement. Sports programmes serve as a positive and productive activity for refugees and internally displaced persons, easing many of the problems they face, including violence, limited access to education and broken family structures. Sport is used as a bridge between refugee and host communities, providing an opportunity for the communities to engage in positive activities. For example, in Thailand, "friendly matches" were coordinated by UNHCR between refugee communities from the Tham Him camp and the local people from Suan Phung.

Former child soldiers: Child soldiers are uprooted from their communities and social structures and experience extreme brutality. The process of their demobilization and rehabilitation is difficult and highly sensitive, requiring physical, psychological and psychosocial care, as well as opportunities to develop the skills necessary for adult life. Here, sport can play a unique role. Sports programmes offer a space to play, giving children back their childhood, while providing an outlet for channelling anger and controlling aggression.

Sports teams also allow these young people to build positive connections with peers and adults, creating a sense of belonging that is essential for their effective demobilization. In Sierra Leone, UNICEF partners with the NGO Right To Play to incorporate sport and play into its Community Based Reintegration programme. Volunteers are working with local communities to build a network of coaches who will implement sports programmes and provide young people with a sense of belonging through the establishment of crucial community connections.

INTERNATIONAL PEACE INITIATIVES

On the global level, sport can serve as a compelling symbol for peace. The United Nations General Assembly recognizes the potential of sport to support the building of a peaceful and better world, and since 1993 has endorsed the Olympic Truce in advance of the Olympic Games. Worldwide, there is increasing recognition of the power of sport as an international messenger for peace. Sport has on several occasions successfully brought together the two Koreas, most recently seen at the 2003 Pan-Asian Games when the North and South Korean teams marched side by side in the opening ceremony.

UEFA began its partnership with ICRC in 1997 when it made resources available for the campaign against landmines. The partnership has expanded to raise funds and awareness concerning the importance of protecting children in war, particularly against their recruitment as child soldiers and for the legal provisions to protect them. The Pakistani-Israeli tennis pair Aisam ul-Haq Quereshi and Amir Hadad served as positive role models for peace within their countries, known globally as "a two-man peace initiative, with rackets". Key considerations regarding sport and peace Given that the skills and values taught through sport are compatible with efforts to promote peace, sports activities should be considered as a supportive element of programmes in post-conflict and high-tension areas. It is imperative that sport-for-peace programmes emphasize the positive values and cohesive potential of sport, and are provided in safe and supportive environments that are enjoyable and pressurefree. Sport-related peace initiatives require responsible and well-trained leadership. As an international language, sport should be considered as a practical means to communicate messages of peace and help find non-violent solutions to problems.

SPORT AND COMMUNICATION

Sport is one of the world's most powerful communication tools due to its near universal appeal, its convening power and its many positive associations.

Together, these features give sport the capacity to reach a range of audiences in a variety of ways, particularly groups that are otherwise difficult to reach. On its own, sport has the ability to communicate messages such as cooperation, coexistence, or how to graciously manage victory and defeat. As a powerful channel to communicate messages, sport can also be an arena to promote United Nations goals for development and peace. Whether a one-time event or a longer-term campaign, sport provides valuable opportunities for both advocacy and the mobilization of communities.

SPORT AND ADVOCACY

Many United Nations organizations successfully collaborate with the world of sport in the area of communications, generating awareness about key issues through global and local efforts. There are various ways to apply sport as a vehicle to send messages, including working with athletes as ambassadors or spokespersons, the dedication of sports events to development issues, the involvement of the media, and collaboration between all partners involved in sports events, including the private sector. These elements can be used individually, or together as part of a coherent communications framework.

The US-based Johns Hopkins University Center for Communication Programs partners with sports associations and health organizations in over 30 African countries to promote healthy lifestyles and behaviours. Health information booths are set up inside stadiums, educational materials are distributed, counselling services are offered, pre-match and half-time forums are held to advocate action, and male and female athletes serve as spokespersons at events and in the media.

Athletes as Goodwill Ambassadors: The popularity of sports stars allows them to effectively reach diverse audiences, as well as attract the media's attention. In addition to raising awareness about issues, athletes serving as spokespersons can generate the interest of fellow athletes and team members, and contribute to resource mobilization efforts. At the global level, UNDP works with footballers Ronaldo and Zinédine Zidane, who act as Goodwill Ambassadors to advocate and support efforts for poverty reduction.

At the local level, UNESCO and UNICEF collaborate in Cambodia to communicate HIV/AIDS prevention messages through a national poster campaign that highlights four well-known athletes in four different sports, including swimming, Khmer boxing, football and running. Sports events: Sports events are an ideal forum for reaching large numbers of people, whether at the event or through its media coverage.

Methods for raising awareness include using public service announcements, in-stadium videos and banners, half-time shows, publications and linkages on event web sites. Globally, sports events can incorporate all of the above elements and provide additional opportunities in marketing and fund-raising.

At the global level, UNICEF and FIFA formed an alliance to promote the "Say Yes for Children" campaign during the 2002 FIFA World Cup in Korea/Japan. Multiple elements were used including public service announcements with footballers, information on child rights in publications and on FIFA's web site and the generation of funds through an auction of sports memorabilia. The alliance also resulted in collaboration between UNICEF country offices and national football federations in over 70 countries. At the community level, the NGO Comvida in Honduras uses national football matches as a communications tool to increase awareness about HIV/AIDS prevention, putting on mock games prior to matches featuring players like "Knowledge" and "Condom" as well as "Infected Syringe" and "Infidelity", representing "Death United".

Within sports organizations: Establishing strong relationships with sports federations and associations is an effective way to tap into existing networks and structures on regional and national levels, allowing a large and diverse audience to be reached with key United Nations messages. As sports organizations work to develop their sport at local levels, United Nations bodies can promote and support those areas where the development of sport overlaps with the use of sport-for-development issues.

Furthermore, working directly with sports organizations can lead to positive changes and get them on board, setting high-profile examples for others to follow. UNEP's work with IOC led to the environment becoming the third dimension of the Olympics—alongside sport and culture—and to the development of guidelines for "green" Olympic Games, with supplementary effects to other sports federations and associations and NOCs. Sports media: The print and broadcast media are further avenues for advocacy through sport. Profiles of individuals who have been affected by sport, accounts that highlight charitable involvement of athletes, or stories that bring light to United Nations sport-related activities raise awareness about development issues.

Campaigns: Many United Nations communications campaigns use sport in a variety of innovative ways: ILO partners with FIFA and the African Confederation of Football (CAF) to promote the "Red Card to Child Labour" campaign, which at the 2002 African Cup of Nations in Mali used sponsors, the media and promotions at matches and national and local football events to spread its message. WHO dedicated 2002 World Health Day to "Move for Health" and 2002 World Tobacco Day to "Tobacco Free Sports" in collaboration with FIVB, FIFA (Tobacco-Free World Cup in Korea/Japan) and IOC (Tobacco-Free Salt Lake City 2002 Winter Olympic Games). UNDP's campaign "Teams to End Poverty" draws upon the advocacy power of sports stars including Ronaldo, Zinédine Zidane, Martina Hingis, Sergey Bubka and Jacques Villeneuve. UNEP's "Play for the Planet" campaign aims to bring young people closer to nature through sport and raise awareness that sport and sports facilities can adversely affect the environment. UNHCR's "Wannabe" campaign in Argentina, Australia, Germany, Greece and Spain uses images of refugee children playing football to create empathy for refugees. UNICEF's alliances with FIFA (2003 Women's World Cup) and Fox Kids (Under-13 Fox Kids Cup) promote "25 by 2005", a campaign for girls' education aiming to get all girls in school and achieve gender parity in education in 25 countries by 2005. UNODC's "Sports against Drugs" public awareness campaign uses sports stars and sports events in over 40 countries to promote positive life choices and a drug-free lifestyle.

SPORT AND SOCIAL MOBILIZATION

Sport is a particularly effective element to support social mobilization efforts. The convening power of sport makes it a useful tool to gather communities for direct public initiatives. It allows for broad delivery of messages and programmes to a wide range of people at the local and national levels, drawing diverse groups of people together in a fun and supportive environment. Whether as an additional element to an existing sports event or as a sports festival specifically organized to support mobilization efforts, sport platforms provide a practical and cost-effective medium to get critical information and programmes to hard-to-reach groups in a comfortable and familiar atmosphere.

In Nairobi, Kenya, the German Population Fund and UN-Habitat ran a football league for homeless young people at risk from prostitution, violence and HIV/AIDS. By gathering together over 1,000 street children, the tournaments offered an entry point for organizations to provide services and support, highlighting the value of providing an enabling environment for sports activities that can then be used as a vehicle for outreach and social mobilization. As a valuable supplement to health initiatives, particularly immunization campaigns, sport platforms are an effective way to bring adults and young people together in a friendly environment. They can attract people into district centres from surrounding regions, and increase the numbers of those reached with critical vaccines.

In Ghana, a sports festival was organized by government ministries, WHO, UNICEF, the Vaccine Fund and Right To Play to mobilize rural communities in order to be immunized with the 5-in-1 vaccine. Over 4,000 people were reached in one day. In Zambia, in June 2003, government ministries, United Nations agencies and NGOs were to use the power of sport as a tool to increase those reached with measles vaccines during a national campaign. This initiative combined a large-scale advertising campaign using one of the country's football stars and local sports events.

KEY CONSIDERATIONS REGARDING SPORT AND COMMUNICATION

Public campaigns should have clear strategies and focused objectives, and consideration should be given to the various ways to use sport as a vehicle to send messages. When designing communications initiatives using sport, programme objectives, target audiences and the media to communicate must be clearly defined. Athletes who serve as spokespersons or ambassadors must reflect the values of the United Nations. Care should be taken when partnering with elite sport for communications purposes given potential conflicts of interest in getting the public and media's attention during "noisy events" and the potential commercialism involved.

At the local and national levels, sport should also be considered as a highly effective tool to support social mobilization efforts and a practical method of engaging diverse communities in broader activities, particularly in support of large-scale immunization campaigns or other health initiatives. Sport and Partnerships

The eighth MDG calls for the establishment of a global partnership for development as a way both to involve new sections of society and to meet global development challenges more effectively.

The sports sector provides a significant opportunity for establishing such new partnerships for development. Partnerships are also a particularly effective way to work with sport, given that the world of sport is by definition a world of partnerships, incorporating diverse actors from the community, the public and private sectors and sports organizations at various scales (see figure 3 below). The implementation of sportfor- development programmes and the use of sport by the United Nations should, therefore, be based upon strategic partnerships with the range of stakeholders involved in sport, coordinated through a common framework.

PARTNERSHIP APPROACH TO SPORT-FOR-DEVELOPMENT PROGRAMMES

There are three areas where a partnership approach to sport for development is especially effective. Programme implementation: Many existing sport-for-development programmes are based on innovative partnerships among actors in the sector, including sports organizations, government authorities, volunteers, and NGOs with specific expertise in implementing sport-related development programmes. UNDP has partnered with NOCs in over 50 countries since 1997 through various initiatives to fight poverty.

WHO works with multiple levels of government in various countries to develop multisectoral policies necessary for effective "Move for Health" initiatives. In numerous countries, including Mozambique and Nicaragua, Universitas, a United Nations programme established by ILO, the Italian Government and a range of UN agencies, is tapping into the international network of universities to assist with the training and management aspects of sport and to actively address issues of knowledge-sharing and youth training in conjunction with efforts to enhance local development through sport.

Resource mobilization: Partnerships provide a strategic approach to resource mobilization, both for and through sport. They are an effective way to fund development initiatives for specific issues, and are useful instruments for government initiatives. Ways to mobilize resources include engaging sports organizations and athletes or forging partnerships and with the private sector. Corporate philanthropy efforts are particularly effective if working with sponsors of major sports events or focusing on cause related marketing or other creative initiatives.

The Olympafrica Foundation funds centres throughout Africa that use sport to foster social development. Olympafrica operates in partnership with major donors including a number of UN agencies and international corporations, as well as community groups and partners at the local level.

In Cuba, there are 41,000 tertiary-educated technical support and training personnel who are sports specialists. These people are a valuable resource in Cuba's technical cooperation programmes in over 100 countries, who can be working alongside medical personnel to address health and social issues through sport. Advocacy: Partnering with the sports world also provides innovative ways to communicate the messages of the United Nations to diverse groups and to effectively mobilize society around certain issues (see "Sport and Communication").

A COMMON FRAMEWORK ON SPORT FOR DEVELOPMENT AND PEACE

A strategic approach should be developed in the United Nations system to foster field-based partnerships related to sport in a way that is both impact-oriented and cost-effective, as well as complementary to technical cooperation projects and broader development goals.

The creation of a common framework on sport for development and peace would draw together the full spectrum of actors involved with sport, including government (e.g. ministries for youth, sport, health, finance and others), sports organizations (e.g. sports federations, NOCs, national football associations, sports clubs), sport-related development NGOs, and the private sector. Within this framework, the resources and needs of particular locations should be mapped, communication and consultation between the different actors facilitated, and strategic actions and partnerships planned.

This common framework must also be combined with the existing planning process of the United Nations to ensure that sport is effectively mainstreamed into United Nations activities. The United Nations system relies on several coordination mechanisms to identify national development priorities (e.g. CCA and UNDAF) and to coordinate their humanitarian and peacekeeping operations. Recipient countries, donors and NGOs also use these instruments to formulate their policies and priorities in the field.

Sport should be incorporated into such coordination instruments, first, to better integrate sportrelated programmes into the United Nations system's broad strategic planning and, second, so that those using these instruments can realize the full value of sport to achieve development and peace promotion objectives.

Establishing this common framework would bring new potential partners into development planning and would add value to existing coordination instruments by providing the expertise and means to use sport effectively in the achievement of the MDGs.

KEY CONSIDERATIONS REGARDING SPORT AND PARTNERSHIPS

A common framework on sport for development and peace should be established at the national level that draws a broad range of actors together in order to create strategic partnerships for programme implementation and assist country-based planning. The world of sport presents a natural partnership for the United Nations system and should be included in the cultivation of a "global partnership for development"—the eighth MDG. Sport provides an innovative avenue to engage civil society into development initiatives.

SPORT AND HIV/AIDS

The HIV/AIDS pandemic is one of the greatest threats to life, dignity and the enjoyment of human rights. UNAIDS estimates that 42 million people are living with HIV/AIDS; 90 per cent are from developing countries, 75 per cent in sub-Saharan Africa.

Fourteen million children have lost one or both parents to the disease. The extent of devastation caused by this pandemic makes it more than a health issue. HIV/AIDS has fundamental implications for economic development, social cohesion and security, which resonate throughout society. Consequently, all aspects of civil society, including sport, must be mobilized in the global fight against HIV/AIDS.

THE IMPACT OF SPORT ON HIV/AIDS

Sport can be a vehicle to help mitigate the spread and impact of HIV/AIDS. The four pillars necessary for effective HIV/AIDS programming are knowledge, life skills, the provision of a safe and supportive environment and access to services.

The nature of sport and the benefits derived when it is incorporated into development initiatives make it well suited to support these four pillars. The groups most at risk of contracting the disease—women and young people, especially girls—are known to be highly responsive to targeted sports initiatives (see "Sport and Social Development").

Knowledge: Coaches and leaders of sports programmes are well placed to incorporate HIV/AIDS prevention activities into sports programmes.

Young people playing sport usually have a special and trusting relationship with their coaches, often unlike other relationships with adults. This puts coaches in a good position to discuss sensitive issues, especially sex, in a way necessary to effectively teach HIV/AIDS prevention and to care for those members who are HIV-positive.

Life skills: Well-designed sports programmes teach essential life skills necessary for HIV/AIDS protection and prevention, further enhancing the effectiveness of incorporating sport (see "Sport and Education").

Studies shows, for example, that when adolescent girls participate in sport, they develop a sense of ownership of and respect for their bodies, encouraging them to delay sexual activity.38 Safe and supportive environment: Given the informal, social and fun nature of sport and play, the playing field can be readily transformed into a secure environment necessary for effective HIV/AIDS programmes and activities.

Sport provides a forum to openly discuss the disease, its transmission and the eradication of stigma and discrimination. In particular, this is especially effective in the care and support of orphans and other vulnerable children, in that sport not only provides structure and connections with others but it also provides a space for expression and a chance to play. Access to services: Sport is well placed to increase knowledge, provide life skills and create a safe environment. It is, therefore, an ideal location to access services, particularly for young people.

Collaboration with sports organizations can tap into an existing network of clubs, volunteers and communication channels, providing a medium to engage large numbers of people quickly.

"Kicking AIDS Out" is a regional network of organizations in southern Africa that uses sport to strengthen communities. It creates sustainable sports activities that increase awareness about HIV/AIDS, provide leadership training to at-risk youth and offer safe and healthy alternative activities.

The effectiveness of sport for communication and social mobilization makes it a highly effective tool for raising public awareness about HIV/AIDS. Sports leagues and matches bring communities together, providing an ideal site for public information campaigns on prevention and protection and reaching large numbers of people of varying backgrounds and ages. Furthermore, sport's positive associations and the widespread perception that it is removed from formal politics means that these messages have the potential to reach populations who might not otherwise be reached.

The participatory nature of sport also makes it a powerful means to dispel misunderstandings about the disease, breaking down stigma and discrimination.

Information about HIV/AIDS is not getting out and is especially not being absorbed by adolescents. Therefore, it is imperative to explore new and innovative ways to deliver prevention messages. The deep roots of sport within communities and its appeal to young people make it a positive forum for implementing HIV/AIDS prevention programmes.

UNFPA supports the Botswana Christian Council and the Botswana National Sports Council as part of its efforts to promote reproductive health and HIV/AIDS prevention among adolescents.

These two societal institutions were chosen because of their significant influence on young people and high levels of youth participation, emphasizing the power of sport to address the issue of HIV/AIDS.

THE IMPACT OF HIV/AIDS ON SPORT

The impact of HIV/AIDS on the world of sport will be dramatic, especially in high-incidence countries.

HIV infection is concentrated among young people and the working-age population, the same groups that are most involved in sport.

Sports organizations in high-incidence countries will increasingly be confronted by the fact that athletes, coaches, staff and members will become ill and die. Already HIV/AIDS absences, due to people becoming ill, attending funerals or caring for sick family members, are eroding many sports bodies and threatening them with organizational collapse. While all organizations in high-incidence countries face this threat, sports organizations, like community-based groups and NGOs, are particularly vulnerable, given that they often rely on people with specialized skills and volunteers who can be difficult to replace.

Faced with this prospect, sports organizations need to plan their response. This can include innovative thinking in the recruitment of new members, staff, coaches and volunteers. However, it should also include working with existing personnel to help prevent the spread of the disease and to mitigate its impact on those who are already infected or personally affected.

HIV-positive sportswomen and sportsmen must feel that they are in "safe havens" in their sports organizations. ILO, with UNAIDS, has developed a "Code of Practice on HIV/AIDS and the World of Work", as well as a "Tool Box for Young Workers on HIV/AIDS", a valuable resource for sports organizations.

KEY CONSIDERATIONS REGARDING SPORT AND HIV/AIDS

Sports organizations and associations should be incorporated into the global fight against HIV/AIDS and actively brought in as partners by the United Nations system. Sports programmes aimed at tackling HIV/AIDS must include all elements necessary for effective HIV/AIDS programming, especially the four pillars: knowledge, life skills, a safe and supportive environment and access to services.

The full capacity of sport-for-development initiatives must be realized on both the international and local levels, for the purposes of raising awareness about the disease, increasing knowledge about prevention and directly tackling stigma and discrimination in a positive, participatory manner. The organizers of sport-based HIV/AIDS prevention programmes should be trained effectively in the issues surrounding HIV/AIDS in addition to sports coaching and how to work with young people. A generic curriculum on HIV/AIDS, for local adaptation, should be elaborated for sports coaches, trainers and others involved in sport.

CONCLUSION AND RECOMMENDATIONS

This report has shown that sport—from play and physical activity to organized and competitive sport— is a powerful and cost-effective way to support development and peace objectives. The many benefits of sport and physical activity are not only enjoyed by the individual, but felt throughout society.

There is, therefore, a crucial need for United Nations agencies, Governments and concerned stakeholders to integrate sport and physical activity into policies and programmes across a range of sectors, including health, education, and economic and social development. By promoting sport in a strategic, systematic and coherent way, the potential of sport as a tool for development and peace can be realized.

When sport is used as an instrument for development and peace it must be implemented in a way that is equity-driven and culturally relevant.

Sports programmes must be based upon the "sport for all" model, ensuring that all groups are given the opportunity to participate, particularly those who gain additional benefits such as women, persons with disabilities and young people. Sports programmes must also be designed explicitly to draw out the core skills and values that can be learned through sport.

When the positive aspects of sport are maximized, it is a powerful and cost-effective way of supporting a range of development and peace objectives. The time is ripe for the United Nations system to realize the full potential of sport as a viable and practical tool for development and peace. The on recommends the following:

1. Sport in the development agenda: Calls for the incorporation of sport and physical activity into the development policies of countries as well as the development agendas of national and international development agencies, with particular emphasis on young people.
2. Sport as a programme tool: Urges Governments and United Nations agencies to include the opportunity to participate in sport as an objective as well as a tool to achieve the Millennium Development Goals and the goals of other international conferences and the broader aims of development and peace.
3. Sport in United Nations country programmes: Recommends the inclusion of sport-related initiatives into the programmes of United Nations agencies, where appropriate and according to locally assessed needs.
4. Partnerships: Recommends that the United Nations system:
   (a) Take a leadership role in fostering dialogue between the worlds of sport and development at the national and international levels in order to facilitate the development of innovative partnerships involving sport for development;
   (b) Consider creating a "global network on sport for development" to facilitate partnerships between the UN system and sport-related organizations, including sports federations and associations and IOC, sport-related humanitarian NGOs, the private sector, athletes and teams and volunteers.
5. Resource mobilization:
   (a) Urges Governments to identify and make available resources for:
      - Sports initiatives, which maximize participation in and access to "sport for all", within their own countries;

- Sport-for-development programmes within overseas development assistance;
- Strengthening the position of sport and physical activity in policy development generally.

(b) Urges United Nations system partners, including private sector partners, sports organizations and civil society, to generate in-kind and financial support for sport for development and peace.

6. Communication: Encourages the United Nations system to seek new and innovative ways to use sport for communication and social mobilization, particularly at the national, regional and local levels, engaging civil society through active participation and ensuring that target audiences are reached.

7

Sports Development Plans

THE AIM OF THE GUIDANCE NOTES

These notes aim to take you through the stages of developing a Sports or Community Development Plan. You can use the headings and format laid out below as a starting point in creating your organisation's Development Plan.

Not every point is relevant to every organisation, but the SCNI believes your organisation should look at all the elements in each section and make an effort to write some detail for each. The SCNI expects the details you provide to reflect the size of your organisation and the level of funding you are requesting.

Each organisation should consult with your local authority Sports Development Officer and/or your governing body development officer when developing this plan. (Contact details for the Sports Development Network are available on our web site www.sportni.net). You may also consider the Coaching NI 'Sports Development Planning' workshop to be useful.

It is important that this document is 'bought into' by your full organisation and is not merely a paper exercise. If you use this plan to assist in your application to 'Building Sport' and you are successful, you will find that the progress of the plan is monitored and tracked by the SCNI. If your are developing this plan along with your application to 'Building Sport' you should consider each of the areas with the relevant sections of the Information Booklet for guidance.

A sub-group of your management committee should develop the Sports Development Plan but your full management committee should feed into and accept the plan. All current and proposed work contributing to the development and success of your club or organisation should be highlighted in this document, with clear responsibilities and timescales. The Sports Development Plan should ideally cover either a three to five year period.

INTRODUCTION AND BACKGROUND

Give a brief history of your organisation including:

- Organisation
- Membership
- Current Facilities
- Management Structure

STRATEGIC CONTEXT

This is a statement of the major external issues affecting the organisation. It will summarise all the key issues facing the organisation and set the scene for the future direction and actions planned.

- Trends in your sport or sports, e.g. increasing participation of young women
- Audit of local situation
- Local organisation membership
- Demographics
- Competition from other similar organisations in your area
- Facilities
- Barriers to your organisation's development
- Deprivation of your catchment area, e.g. Noble Deprivation Indices

- Skill base in the area, e.g. previous experience of project management
- Consultation findings, e.g. community audit, club, governing body etc
- Opportunities for coaching, participation and performing
- Partner and stakeholders working with the organisation.

What are the positive/negative external forces influencing your operation?

- Local Authority policies and plans in your area
- Sports Council policies and strategic plans in your sport and area
- Education and Library Board policies and plans
- Health and Social Service Board policies and plans
- Funding opportunities for your organisation
- Central Government policies, e.g. Department of Culture, Arts and Leisure
- Governing Body policies and plans in your sport and area

WHERE IS THE ORGANISATION NOW?

What are the strengths and weaknesses in your present operation?

Remember to take into account any existing development, operational or performance plans which you may have and your resources, both in terms of finance and people.

Areas that should be considered:

- Do current facilities meet your users' requirements?
- Do current facilities allow access and use for all?
- Does your management committee have the capacity/ expertise to meet the demands of the club and the conditions funders expect them to meet? E.g. project management, financial, technical or sports development experience

- Are there a sufficient number of coaches to meet the requirements of all members?
- What is the trend of active members over the last number of years?
- Are all categories of users catered for? E.g. women, children, people with a disability, people of differing cultures and ethnic backgrounds
- Is the club operating under a current Sports Development Plan and how is it progressing?
- What links do you have with local schools/community groups in your area?
- Has your organisation been successful in promoting sport over the last number of years?
    - o If yes, what are the reasons for this?
    - o If no, what factors have caused the poor success of your teams or individuals?

WHERE DOES YOUR ORGANISATION WANT TO BE?

Give a vision statement illustrating the main aims of the organisation over the coming period. Identify your organisation's main strategic objectives over the next 3 to 5 years.

Your objectives should be SMART, i.e.:

Specific, Measurable, Achievable, Relevant, Timebound

Some examples of strategic/SMART objectives are listed below, they may not all be relevant to your situation, but:

1. To increase the number of: women, men, young people, people with disabilities, and people from different religious, cultural and ethnic backgrounds participating in sport through your organisation from [number] to [number] by the end of the [1st/2nd/3rd] year of the project.
2. Set up a junior [insert sport] team(s) by the end of year one.

3. Set up junior/female league structures by the end of year two.
4. To increase the performance of individuals, teams and the organisation by competing/winning [name of competition/event] by the end of the [1st/2nd/3rd] year of the project.
5. To increase the number of coaching opportunities from [number] to [number] in the [1st/2nd/3rd] year of the project.
6. To develop [number] existing coaches to level 1/2/3 coaching in your identified courses.
7. To employ a new sports development officer/coach by the end of the [1st/2nd/3rd] year of the project.
8. To increase membership of your organisation from [number] to [number] through marketing, promotion and success of the club by the end of the [1st/2nd/3rd] year of the project.
9. To establish formal links with [number] of primary schools and [number] post primary schools by the end of the [1st/2nd/3rd] year of the project.
10. To establish formal links with [number] other community groups and formal sports clubs and [number] post primary schools by the end of the [1st/2nd/3rd] year of the project.
11. To increase the financial health and viability of the club by setting up a fundraising committee in the 2nd month of your project.

HOW WILL WE GET THERE?

What actions have to take place to achieve the strategic/SMART objectives?

It is likely the strategic objectives can only be achieved through a number of actions being taken.

These actions may include:

- Carry out a needs analysis of the local community to find out what facilities the local community require and would like to meet their needs.
- Carry out an access audit of your organisations current facilities, and make all suggested changes.
- Develop a Sports Development Plan.
- Develop formal links with local schools, community and voluntary groups and local sports clubs to make best usage of your facilities.
- Adopt child protection, equity, health and safety, equal opportunities policies.
- Training of management committee in finance, project management, sports development etc.
- Members to achieve coaching awards, eg. Sport for All Leader Award.
- Long Term Athlete Development programme to be introduced.
- Employment of a Sports Development Officer.
- Development of a business plan.
- Development of a female and youth sports section.
- Construction of new playing facilities (pitch, court, alley, sports hall etc.)
- Construction of new changing facilities.
- Renovation of current facilities.
- Purchase of land to develop facilities.
- Purchase of equipment.

How will you measure the success of your organisation against your objectives?

Systems to monitor and record the following information should allow your club to monitor its success in achieving the strategic objectives.

Looking at some of the following can help monitor actual performance against objectives:

- Number of individuals participating from each section of society
- Number of participants from under-represented groups
- Number of teams participating
- Attendance of members at training and competition
- Increase in the number of individuals from each section of the community identified joining the club
- Number of new coaches at each level working with playing members
- Increased success of the organisation's teams
- Increased success of individuals from the organisation in competition
- Number of club players involved in governing body representative squads
- Financial position of the organisation in accessing funding
- Increased awareness of the activities of the organisation

ACTION PLAN TABLE

The table below may be useful for you to summarise the information you will provide in sections 4-6.

It is helpful both for members to see at a glance the organisation's plan for the coming seasons, but also for external agencies such as SCNI or other potential funders to understand clearly, with targets, what your organisation plans to do. If you like, sections 1-3 'set the scene', and sections 4-6 describe the future of the organisation.

Objective	Actions	Responsibility	Timescale	Output	Measures
Here you should detail the main objectives of your organisation for the 3-5 year period as in section 4 above	Here you should detail the actions required to deliver each objective. You may find that each objective has more than one action required (section 5 above)	Who will be responsible for ensuring that the actions are taken?	When do you plan each action to start, or by when should it have been achieved?	What is the output of the successful action e.g. number of users increases from 120 to 200 per week	How will you measure the successes e.g. by a signing in book, team lists etc.

SUMMARY ON SPORTS FOR DEVELOPMENT

Sport, recreation and play are a fun and engaging way to learn values and lessons that will last a lifetime.

They promote the spirit of friendship, solidarity and fair play. They teach teamwork, self-discipline, trust, respect for others, leadership and coping skills - essential to ensuring that children develop into responsible and caring individuals. They help prepare young people to meet the challenges they will face and to take leadership roles within the communities.

Regular physical activity and play are essential for physical, mental, psychological and social development from early childhood through adolescence.

Involvement in sports can boost children's confidence and help reduce symptoms of stress and depression. Studies have shown that participation in sports can improve academic performance, prevent smoking and alcohol and drug abuse, and help reduce crime. Sports can have particular benefits for girls by breaking down gender stereotypes. Sport festivals and games are used to educate families about health issues, including the need for vaccination and HIV/

AIDS prevention. Sport is an effective way to reach children and adolescents who are often excluded and discriminated against, including orphans, disabled children, street children, former child soldiers, sexually exploited children and children from indigenous communities.

The level of detail provided in the Sports Development Plan should be commensurate with the scale of the project and the level of funds requested from SNI. Projects which require a higher level of award, such as synthetic pitches, should have a range of community partners and should be marketed to a wider catchment area. These projects would be expected to provide a robust response to all questions, and demonstrate significant user numbers and partnerships.

If you have additional detail under each of the questions, please feel free to add additional bullet points. It is important that you give as much information as possible about the sports development impact of your project through this plan.

SPORTS DEVELOPMENT PLAN

1a. As a result of this project what actions will you undertake over the next five years to increase participation in sport within your organisation?

	Current	Year 1*	Year 2	Year 3	Year 4	Year 5
Adult Male						
Adult Female						
Junior Male						
Junior Female						
Totals						

* *Year on year figures should be additionality not an accumulation*

1b. As a result of the actions identified above in 1a, please list the total number of participants expected to participate in sport at the project over the five years following completion of the project.

2a. Some groups of people are under represented in sport. For recording purposes SNI prioritises:

- Females
- People with a Disability
- Ethnic Minority groups
- People who are aged over 50

As a result of this project, what actions will you put in place to involve more of these groups in sport in your organisation over the 5 years?

2b. As a result of the actions identified above in 2a, please list the total number of participants within the identified groups expected to participate in sport at the project over the five years following completion of the project.

	Current	Year 1	Year 2	Year 3	Year 4	Year 5
Females						
Those with a Disability						
Ethnic Minorities						
Aged over 50						

3a. How will you improve the quality of coaching and the coaching structures at your organisation over the five years, and in particular how will you increase the total number of coaches taking coaching sessions at your project? Please be specific about the qualifications, the level and the sport (especially for multi sport applications). You should ensure that you have sufficient and appropriately qualified coaches in place to enable work with a range of under represented groups such as people with disabilities, and young people.

	Current	Year 1	Year 2	Year 3	Year 4	Year 5
Male						
Female						
Total number of coaches						
Coaches with a Disability						
Coaches aged over 50						

	Current	Year 1	Year 2	Year 3	Year 4	Year 5
Male						
Female						
Total number of coaches						
Coaches with a Disability						
Coaches aged over 50						

3b. As a result of the actions identified above in 3a, please list the expected number of coaches/leaders/instructors that will coach at least once at your project during each of the next five years. This can include coaches who attend summer schemes but are not necessarily regular coaches within the club.

3c. As a result of the actions identified above in 3a, please list the number of people you expect to have attained qualifications or attended a coach development/leadership course at your project over the five years following completion of the project.

4a. What actions will you take to improve the volunteering capacity within your organisation over the next five years?

4b. As a result of the actions identified above in 4a, please list the number of expected volunteers to be involved through the project over the five years following completion of the project.

	Current	Year 1	Year 2	Year 3	Year 4	Year 5
Male Volunteers						
Female Volunteers						
Total No of volunteers						

5a. What planned initiatives (if any) has your organisation in place for performance athletes and Governing Body development squads over the next five years? These may be targets or actions which have been developed in conjunction with your Governing Body or local schools.

5b. As a result of the actions identified above in 5a, please list the expected number of high performance athletes participating at your project over the five years following completion of the project.

6a. There are a number of other Key Performance Indicators which may also be able to impact with this project. Please note any actions which you will take that will assist with the development of the following:

- Health Referrals – The number of individual referrals from a health professional to your proposed project who take part until the end of the prescribed course.

	Current	Year 1	Year 2	Year 3	Year 4	Year 5
Male Athletes						
Female Athletes						
Total No of Athletes						

- Young People at Risk – The number of young people aged under 25 who are 'at risk', who take part in structured activity sessions lasting over 6 weeks or more.
- Sports Jobs – The number of full-time equivalent permanent (12 months or more) jobs created or safe guarded in your project or organisation by your project.
- Funding – The additional investment that your project has secured for sport and physical activity *after* it started.

	Current	Year 1	Year 2	Year 3	Year 4	Year 5
Health Referrals						
Young People at Risk						
Sports Jobs						
Additional capital investment generated						

6b. As a result of the actions identified above in 6a, please list the number of expected initiatives to impact on the following areas over the five years following completion of the project.

In October 2002, the United Nations Secretary General convened an Inter-Agency Task Force to review activities involving sport within the United Nations system.

The Task Force, co-chaired by UNICEF Executive Director Carol Bellamy, produced *Sport for Development and Peace: Towards Achieving the Millennium Development Goals.*

The comprehensive report concluded that sport is a powerful and cost-effective way to advance the Millennium Development goals, the agenda agreed to by world leaders at the UN Millennium Summit and the World Fit for Children.

In November 2003, the United Nations General Assembly adopted a resolution on the role of sport as a means to promote health, education, development and peace, proclaiming 2005 as the International Year for Sport and Physical Education.

UNICEF recognizes the critical role of sport and physical activity in children's lives.

Not only are sports and recreation means to achieve UNICEF's core objectives, they are goals in themselves to ensure every child's right to play. Every child has a right to a healthy start in life; every girl and boy a right to be educated; and every adolescent to have ample opportunity to develop into caring and involved citizens.

UNICEF is using sports as a tool to promote health, education, development and peace.

With our partners, UNICEF is incorporating opportunities for sport, recreation and play into country programmes to reach children, families and communities around the world. In countries at peace and at war, these activities are being used to promote good health and warn about the harmful affects of alcohol, smoking and other drug use. They are educating young people on the dangers of HIV/ AIDS and empowering them with skills to protect themselves. Sport and recreational programmes are creating environments that are safe and promote stable relationships between children and adults and between children and their peers.

They are providing children of all ages, opportunities to express themselves, contribute their voice, opinions and ideas, and become agents for change. They are helping to rebuild lives and communities and are contributing to a more just and peaceful society.

8

Sports Quotes

INTRODUCTION

Since our first course, we have constantly been told about the 'the sport of speaking', and how it could help us to view our recoveries as a sport. If this sports mentality is to be effective, is there anything we can use to support this, to add structure to our coaching and in turn, eventually achieve better results within the programme in general?

As a Sports Scientist and Sports Coach, I believe that there is a great deal of unlocked potential within sports psychology and the way that we coach and support one another. The purpose of this article is to explore the dynamics of Sports Psychology and attach relevant Sports Coaching principles to them, giving us some guidelines on how to introduce these concepts into our phone-list, 'in-line' and primary coaching.

The aspects of sports psychology to be considered are; motivation, leadership, visualisation, positive re-enforcement, self confidence/self efficacy, stress management, competition, personality type, aggression and musical inspiration. We will also be looking at sports quotes, and how a course instructor may use them.

Motivation

As a stammerer, to gain eloquent speech is one of the biggest motivations. Some of us though, occasionally need an extra push to do those additional contacts, to make those phone calls, or in a more general sense, to continue expanding our comfort zones.

Athletes and their coaches are always aiming higher. Sport and success demands the bar of competition to be constantly raised, causing sports people to run faster, jump higher and throw further. In the endless pursuit of excellence and sporting glory, how does a coach keep their athlete motivated to put in long hours on cold February mornings when the 'stay in bed' option seems very tempting?

One technique widely used within sport is Goal Setting. England and Newcastle Falcons rugby player Jonny Wilkinson is widely renowned as the best player in the world in his position. Wilko is always setting goals, but interestingly, he divides them into two different categories. The first is training goals, looking at aspects such as sprint times, weights lifted, and kicking targets made, the second is competition goals, tackles made, kicks scored and yards gained in a game situation.

We can set goals for ourselves and our students, make 100 contacts per day, phone 3 stronger graduates of the programme each week, 1 hang-up drill per day, use 5 instances for deliberate disfluency at work per day, or simply to phone our primary coach more often. The list is endless, but there are a few principles that we must be aware of. Goal Setting can be counter-productive if not used correctly. If the goals set are too difficult, for the graduate at a specific stage in their recovery, the goals in question will not be achieved. This failure may result in negative thoughts and therefore negative feelings towards the programme and the coach themselves.

The goals should be made as specific as possible, either to the graduate in question or to the speech situation in hand. It is pointless to set a goal of 100 contacts per day, if contacts do not challenge you. You would achieve the goal quickly and easily and defeat the object of the goal setting exercise. It would be better to maybe try 5 walk-away drills per day, or heavy use of Deliberate Disfluency in the post office queue. I believe that the key word here is 'challenge'.

We as coaches, can work with students and use goal setting to improve outcomes of their contact sessions and in general recovery. If one were to take the street contacts on their first course for example, the overall goal is clear, the magical figure of 100. Within those contacts, the coach can break down numbers and set smaller goals, sprint drill for 20 contacts, 10 phone calls, 15 disclosures, 20 block releases, 20 long hit and holds, the possibilities are endless. Setting these goals will make the 100 contacts seem far less daunting for some new students, and may aid to break up the afternoon for the coaches. In the student's recovery, make an attempt to give them small, daily goals at first, small but challenging, then increase the time scale and difficulty as they improve and their confidence grows. Remember, no one knows your students like their primary coach.

Leadership

In sport, leadership is everything to a team or group. Take the England Rugby World Cup Winning side for example, it was captained by Martin Johnson, but he was supported by many leaders, players who captained their club sides, such as Lawrence Dallaglio of London Wasps, Phil Vickery of Gloucester, Jason Robinson of Sale Sharks and of course, Jonny Wilkinson of Newcastle Falcons. I believe that the leadership qualities offered by these players were pivotal to the overall squad's success.

We can transfer good leadership skills to our speech coaching and to our own recoveries. Good leaders are strong, firm, but compassionate communicators, they lead by example, and will guide and support whenever is necessary. There is much call for us all to be good leaders when coaching. We all look to the course instructor when sitting in lines during a course, but it is coaches who can see where the strengths and weaknesses of the new students lie, and can therefore, act effectively upon it.

When in lines, the coach must be a leader by example, disciplined and supportive. The coach has the opportunity to guide the new student through the early stages of their recovery, and then take a leadership role when out on Saturday contacts, overseeing, supporting and helping when necessary, taking the initiative where needed. Leadership responsibilities also rest on the Primary Coache's shoulders after the course, guiding the new graduate through the early steps along freedom's road.

Visualisation

This is one of the most effective methods of sports psychology, difficult to grasp entirely, but when used effectively, can aid in mental preparation, stress reduction and relaxation. If I was to write about this 20 years ago, I'd have made no sense, because I would have only been 4 years old, but seriously, no one had really ever used visualisation in sport.

Today, visualisation is widely used by amateur and elite level performers alike. One of the pioneers of this technique was the Champion Skier, Jean-Claude Killy, who would study a down hill course from video and pictures, and be able to ski it in his mind prior to the race, naturally giving him the advantage on race day. American athlete, Michael Johnson, world record holder at 200 and 400 meter sprints, would mentally rehearse an entire race before entering the starting blocks, knowing where he would fatigue and preparing himself for it, thus reducing stress levels when the event happened during the race itself. World number one Golfer Vijay Singh, is quoted as using visualisation to relax him during a high pressure putt. He said that he often blocks out the crowd around the green, imagining that he is on the practice green at his home golf club, this takes all pressure out of the action itself, allowing his muscles to remain relaxed and able to produce a smooth putting stroke.

The visualisation possibilities for the McGuire Technique are endless. It is already used by many, including myself in many areas, but what some people do not realise is that we have all used it at one point or another, when practicing kinaesthetics - the hand and arm motion that we all use is to mimic the movement of our costal diaphragm when speaking and/or breathing. How can we enhance our use of visualisation?

When in a stressful situation, such as a meeting room introduction or presentation at school, college, or work, we can try and visualise ourselves in support group, or on a course, helping us to concentrate on our speech, rather than the stresses that we put ourselves under in these situations.

We can use mental rehearsal, and use it with our new students/ graduates, during contacts. If they can foresee a problem word or situation prior to going for a contact, simply take them to one side, and talk about what they expect will happen. Then, ask them to close their eyes, imagine themselves encouraging, the contact, feeling confident, and diaphragm moving smoothly and their voice coming from deep in the chest. Then, ask them to attack the contact with the same feelings that they have just been experiencing in their mind, it should help.

In the first year of my recovery, I was a student in the second year of a 2 year HND course. I had put all the presentations off in the first year, so I had no choice but to do them in the second year or fail the course. Presentations were still a feared situation for me, so I asked my lecturers to be excused prior to my presentation slot, they supportively obliged and I used this time to breathe, centre and clarify and prepare for my speech. I visualised my diaphragm moving smoothly, and remembered how it felt to be on the soapbox for the first time. I took those feelings into the presentations, and every one was a success, from the point of view of my speech anyway!

Positive Re-enforcement and Self Talk

Positive thinking is very effective in sport. It can be allied with the phrases 'will to win' and 'playing to win'. There are too many examples in sport to draw upon to illustrate this point, but how many times have a side gone into the changing room at half time during a game, losing to a seemingly insurmountable score line, and then came out for the second half, looking positive, psyched-up and turned the game on it's head?

What does the coach say to the players to restore self belief and confidence? I firmly believe that all negatives have a positive, somewhere, if you look hard enough for it. There is always a glimmer of hope in the most dire of situations, and someone who can tap into that positivity, is going to have a massive advantage.

We all know the importance of staying and thinking positive in our speech and recovery, that's why we all have our soap box pictures and have a positive thinking talk our courses. We should all know how to be positive as coaches, but new graduates may find it hard. An example of this would be a new graduate who has had a bad experience during their day's contacts. An easy way to turn this into a positive would be to speak to them about their experience, and ask them if you would have had the courage to put themselves in that situation to begin with, prior to their first course. The examples are endless.

Positivity is very important, but occasionally forgotten when teaching in the lines. We need to commend, recommend and commend the new students; you may have heard it called the thick sandwich coaching method. It is taken straight out of the sports coaching handbooks, like a tennis serve for example. You may hear a coach say to his athlete, "Great ball toss, try and get your follow through faster, but a solid foot position – well done", surrounding constructive criticism with praise, this really does work at maintaining a positive outlook to the learning process.

Self Confidence and Self Efficacy

How much can I write about sport and confidence? At the highest level, confidence can make or break an athlete's performance in competition. You hear and read in the media, "This players on top of his game, he's in fine touch, he's hearing the music", this means that he has high levels of confidence. It is a simple fact that athletes at the highest standard are of similar skills levels, but the thing that makes a batsman score a century, or a footballer bend a ball around the wall to score a free kick, or a golfer sink a putt to win the Ryder Cup, is high levels of self confidence.

A subdivision of Self Confidence is Self Efficacy. This can be described as situational self confidence, the confidence that an individual had within a single situation or action. Take the sporting example of a hurdler, his technique over he hurdles is fine, but he loses time during the flat running in between, this will lead to his hurdling efficacy being higher than the efficacy of his running.

The relation to our speech and our recovery here is clear for us to see. Confidence, for me in any case, is everything, when something has knocked my confidence in my speech, I do struggle and it takes a lot of work to get my confidence back. We all have our own stories, but self efficacy and our recovery is the important one, I know that my self efficacy in public speaking is high, but my self efficacy on the phone leaves a great deal to be desired. This is something for me to work on, but it is our responsibility as coaches, to evaluate our students and work to increase level of confidence and efficacy in all situations, this will help us to evaluate our own recovery as well.

Stress Management

We all encounter stress in it's many forms. What does it feel like to know that the drop kick you are about to do could win the Rugby World Cup, or this next putt could win you £1 million, or your penalty can put England through in a shoot-out, for a change? Stressful... but the key to success is controlling those stressful feelings to a manageable level.

Too much stress is undoubtedly a bad thing, and can have a detrimental effect on performance, but all stress is not necessarily a bad thing. If I were about to give a public speech, or take a sports coaching session without feeling a little nervous, then I should be worrying about getting complacent with either my speech itself, or the content.

A little stress keeps us on our toes, reminds us all to costal breathe and not get ahead of ourselves. There are many stress management techniques used within sport and the McGuire Programme, and everyone has their own way of doing this. Try to ensure however, that you let your new graduate know about the stress levels that they may encounter in the early stages of their recovery, and how they may control them. Personally, I always keep it simple, close my eyes and costal breathe, visualising my diaphragm moving smoothly.

Competition

What does an athlete train for? What do we drill, exaggerate and follow directions for? To compete with the opposition and to beat the opposition.

I look at every single speaking situation as a game with my stammer, I simply do not play to lose. I look at regular contacts as league games, public speeches, disclosures and interviews as cup finals.

We all have our own mindset when it comes to competition, and some people do not like to view their speech as a big match, but it works for me, so whatever you do, share it with you new graduate, it may help them to contextualise their recovery and put things into greater perspective.

Never forget, that we should never play to lose, when it's you and your stammer, you can only play to win, if you don't want to win, you shouldn't have started the training.

Personality Type

Everyone is different, as is their stammer and the way that it has affected their lives. Your personality type depicts who you are, and how you respond to instruction and coaching. All sports people are different, the most elite athletes are those who make sacrifice, they are dedicated, they know what they want and they will stop at nothing to have the best chance of getting it.

There are also many people in the sporting world, who will attach themselves to teams and groups of people for status and social reasons, they don't like playing on a wet, cold January afternoon, but they enjoy a few drinks with their team-mates after the game. Do these people really want success, and do they really have the commitment to achieve it?

Sir Clive Woodwood had a 6 year plan to winning the Rugby World Cup in 2003. Throughout the build-up, he had his plan; he knew what players he wanted to have at the centre of the world cup winning squad, and the coaching staff who were right for the job.

Take the example of Jason Robinson, who at the start of Sir Clive's reign as England head coach, was a Wigan and Great Britain Rugby League superstar. Sir Clive had always spoke of his admiration of the country's best League players and in 2001, with the help of the Sale Sharks and the Rugby Football Union, convinced Jason Robinson to switch codes to Rugby Union.

Robinson's impact was immediate, he was in the England and British Lions squad by the end of that year, scoring tries almost at will. Sir Clive's plan was working, and finally, in the World Cup final, Jason Robinson scored England's only try of the game, helping the side to eventually win. Sir Clive has now resigned as England coach, but the new coaching staff have named Jason Robinson as England's Captain for 2004's autumn internationals, sealing the importance of Sir Clive's decision and attitude.

Sir Clive is an example that we can all learn from, if we want something enough, plan and work towards it, we have every chance of succeeding in our goal. Eloquence is our goal, in the pursuit of this, we must all be committed, work hard and follow directions, but we also have a considerable obligation to our students, to help, support and enthuse them. Whatever their personality type, they can achieve their goals, but they will need the support of a coach to give them a helping hand along the way.

Aggression

When someone says, "Think of an aggressive sportsman", who do you think of? Vinnie Jones, Roy Keane? Funny how it's normally footballers isn't it? In some sports, control aggression can be a valuable asset to any player, such as ice hockey for example. But I believe that this is one area of sports psychology that has no place in our recovery. I believe that aggression may have been a feeling that some of us may have experienced as out-of-control-stammerers, but why hang on to those feelings now that life has improved? Aggression will lead to excessive levels of ill-feeling, therefore leading to stress, and too much, as I have already covered in this article, is what we as recovering stammerers need to avoid.

Assertiveness is something that we may find useful, but it is something that our new graduates may find difficult to grasp at first. Assertiveness is, although closely linked, entirely different from aggressiveness. We must talk with the new students and graduates about any feelings that they may have, and turn any aggression into something more positive and more controlled.

Musical Inspiration

I believe that everyone should have a feel good song, when you hear it, it makes you smile. I have what I call McGuire Songs, songs that inspire me, and help to get me into the right frame of mind when my hexagon may be imbalanced. My personal songs are linked with my sports background; these are songs that I could have listened to in my changing room before a game, to help me to focus my thoughts. My songs of choice are; 'Beautiful Day' by U2, 'Free' by The Lighthouse Family, 'With arms wide open', and 'Here with me', by Creed, 'Search for the Hero', by M People and 'Proud', by Heather Small. How many people were expecting to see 'Eye of the

Tiger' - I'm afraid that is one step too far! Some people may be looking at that list and thinking why, but those are my choices that inspire me personally.

'Proud', by Heather Small is a particularly powerful song, it was used by Team GB in the 2000 and 2004 Olympic Games, the words are very powerful, and I feel that they are very appropriate to the Saturday of a course. I have done a number of positive thinking sessions, and at the start, I ask the new students to close their eyes, listen to the song, and think about what they had achieved during the day. The reaction from them is quite surprising. Maybe we should all take a moment to think about what our inspirational song should be?

Sports Quotes

People in sport have been saying some very profound things for many years. Some quotes can really sum up what we sometimes find difficult to put into words ourselves.

On my courses, I stick the quotes around the walls of the teaching room; people can read them, be inspired by them and remember them.

One of my personal favourites is by a man called Charles Finlay, "Sweat, plus sacrifice, equals success", I feel that this really sums up the work ethic of the McGuire Programme, that we must work hard, and put ourselves first, to really be good at the sport of speaking. Below, are some of my favourite sporting quotes.

"The price of success is hard work, dedication to the job at hand, and the determination that whether we win or lose, we have applied the best of ourselves to the task at hand." - *Vince Lombardi*

"You have to expect things of yourself before you can do them." - *Michael Jordan*

"The best and fastest way to learn a sport is to watch and imitate a champion." - *Jean-Claude Killy*

"The difference between a successful person and others is not a lack of strength, not a lack of knowledge, but rather a lack of will." - *Vincent Lombardi*

"Champions aren't made in the gyms. Champions are made from something they have deep inside them - a desire, a dream, a vision." - *Muhammad Ali*

In a sporting context, these quotes have been used to great effect. In the England Rugby Squad's changing room and warm up area, there are many quotes pinned up around the walls. But on the door, is a very important one, the same quote also hangs on the door of the English and European Champions, London Wasps', changing room. "Winning is why we are here".

We are all winners in my opinion, to achieve what we all have, is something to be very proud of, but if we want to keep winning, and help other graduates, young and old, to win, sports psychology can offer a great deal to all of us.

9

On Ethics, Journalism, Blogging and a Brave New World of Media

INTRODUCTION

Recently, there's been a lot of coverage in the news about ethics and transparency in the blogging world. Let me give you an example - TechCrunch's Mike Arrington lambasted Wired Magazine recently for an article trashing Digg, when Wired's owner, Conde Naste, owns Digg competitor Reddit. Robert Scoble has come under fire for accepting paid speaking gigs and travel from sponsors. Sony came under fire for suggesting that they would pull all their media support from Kotaku.com, which published an unauthorised story about the PS3.

The world of journalism, blogging and ethics is an interesting, and complicated one. Transparency and ethical reporting have always been issues in the world of mainstream journalism, to a greater or lesser extent. Most established publications have rules on what is and isn't allowed in terms of journalist's activities. But the world is changing. Journalists are becoming bloggers, bloggers are becoming journalists, and blogs are becoming brands.

The internet is bringing people into the world of written reporting who have had no training, have no one to learn from, no sense of their place in the reporting ecosystem. This causes issues all over the place. I've seen so much written lately that completely misunderstands this topic, so I wanted to lay some things out for people so that they can have a better understanding of how reporting works and the criteria for ethical and unethical reporting. First, a little about me. I am a graduate in Law, and my writing career began on the web, writing and self-publishing a website called bit-tech.net.

Through my writing work there I landed a number of paid editorial positions at professional magazines and websites. I have learned on-the-job from respected editors and been fortunate to experience the editorial culture in a diverse range of publications.

Bit-tech is now a professional operation that has editors, offices, sales staff and an established editorial culture. (I have since left for a new venture). Having done the self-published blogging thing as well as the paid journalist and Editor thing, I hope that this qualifies me to write this piece in a way that will be fair to all parties. What are journalist's ethics?

The promotion of 'ethics' in journalism is something fundamental to the profession. It centres around one basic tenet - editorial writing in the free press should be 'independent'. That is, what you are reporting should be truthful and accurate. Editorial should not be 'bought' by companies. Readers should be able to read an article and know that it is your honest work.

All sorts of guidelines and rules are established by different publications in order to secure this independence, to a greater or lesser extent, since editorial independence is traditionally regarded as a necessary condition for commercial and critical success. Let's get one thing clear, however - there are (almost) no blanket rules.

There is no great code of conduct written in stone that journalists and publishers should adhere to. Publications choose their own rules in the hopes of best serving their readers. Why no generally accepted rules? Because reporting often involves compromise, and the degree of compromise acceptable will often vary across audiences. At this point, it is useful to distinguish journalism from publishing, so as to understand the true meaning of journalist ethics. A journalist is a writer, a provider of editorial. Journalists, in the truest (or oldest, take your pick) sense, have little or nothing to do with the creation and management of a publication.

No journalist in the New York Times has a vested interest in seeing advertising sold or readership grown, beyond a very basic level of job security. Traditional publications, run as businesses, are split in half, with the business and advertising team on one side and the editorial team on another. This is the closet thing to a ubiquitous or golden rule in traditional publishing.

The line between them is often referred to as a Chinese wall - nothing should pass between it. This is to prevent business staff from pressuring journalists – making sure that a product gets a good review to secure some advertising budget, for example.

In some offices, the two sets of staff work on different floors, or even in different buildings, and are not even allowed to talk to each other. This is considered fundamental to the operation of most big magazines and newspapers offline, and is one of the main ways in which publishers seek to attain the independence being sought. Why now? And this is one reason that the issue of ethics and integrity has been in the press so much recently - these walls are breaking down and the lines between editorial and business are getting more blurry in many publications.

Why is this? One of the reasons is that the internet has allowed a new generation of writers to self-publish, creating their own blogs and their own brands.

Many blogs and online publications are sustained by just a couple of people, managing their own editorial schedules, their own advertising sales, their own readership growth. Some of them are very successful. I'm going to highlight PerezHilton.com as an example of a one-man publishing brand. Perez has ultimate responsibility for commercial sales, writes all the editorial himself, and has 100% control of his publication. It flies in the face of traditional publishing principles. One could argue that TechCrunch.com is the same, to a degree - whilst Mike Arrington has an editorial team writing for him, many of the big stories are broken by him and most of the ad sales are handled through him.

This is an example of a big, prominent publication in a sector completely flying in the face of the traditional Chinese Wall of publishing. Here's the thing - both PerezHilton.com and TechCrunch.com are fantastic publications.

They are amazing resources in their sectors. I read both every day and love them. So clearly, the traditional Chinese Wall model of publishing and independence isn't the only one that can result in success, in this net-based day and age.

These guys prove that self-publishing can yield both fantastic editorial and commercial success that keeps readers happy. But they also have to establish their own rules about what they consider appropriate in terms of mixing the two roles, and these rules are not as established or accepted as the ones that have operated for years in print land.

This is why they are frequently controversial. Not only are the rules changing in terms of self-publishing, but the web has created a global platform for publishers, in a world where what is considered ethical often varies across borders. I have seen American journalists look on aghast as British journalists recant their benefits. But British journalists and bloggers are now reaching an American audience, and vice versa.

How do you harmonise good ethical practice across the world? I want to look at a few examples of recent issues that have come up in the blogosphere in the hope of providing some interesting analysis of these issues, and perhaps even pointing towards a basic way forwards. Free trips, junkets. Here's a big one. Should journalists accept travel from companies that they are writing about? Answers to this vary greatly, both on and offline, and the answer is not a simple one by any means. Let's take an example: Company A is holding a three day expo of its products half way across the world.

Company A offers to provide plane tickets and accommodation for Journalist B, who works for Publication C. What should be done to be ethical? Journalist B wants to write about Company A, since the company's products are relevant to his Publication, C. But if he accepts the tickets and accommodation, can his writings be considered independent, given that he's basically on a free trip across the world paid for by the company he's writing about? Perhaps Publication C decides that this is beyond what they are prepared to accept as independent. What are their options?

Well, they can prevent Journalist B from going, period - but that's not great, since it would deny their readers coverage of a big event, and that's not good for the readers. So how about paying for the journalist to travel themselves? That's an ideal situation, allowing for coverage without jeopardising independence. But that's tough - given the number of expos and trade shows in a year, the company might soon be pretty bankrupt if it flew journalists around the world all year long, unless it's a long established publication with some big coffers.

What answers are there? Well, what about if Company A offers to buy a large amount of advertising space in Publication C around the time of the expo? A boost in advertising sales would give C some more budget to fly B out to the show.

But is that really much different that A simply offering to fly B out, except that the money goes through the business channel of C? This is a common situation that I have heard discussed time and time again. The New York Times Code of Conduct says that for A to fly B out is not allowed, and if the expo is important enough, C should pay for B to cover it, full stop. This, it reasons, is the only way to guarantee independent editorial - and in the long run, this will bring more readers, which will bring more advertisers, which will cover the costs of the policy at least theoretically.

Many other US publications operate the same way, with journalists not allowed to accept trips anywhere. In the UK, the situation is somewhat different. I have personally accepted trips to America on a number of occasions, not least from Intel, which holds a Developer Forum every six months in San Francisco and regular invites me to stay there for a week and cover the show. There is usually a contingent of 10 British journalists both from newspapers, websites and magazines covering the event and this is considered normal. US journalists invited to the Forum are often expected to pay their own way. What is the correct way to remain ethical? Is there even a correct answer? Probably not a single one, no. What is correct really comes down to what you expect your readership to think. If I take a trip out to IDF with Intel, are my readers going to expect my coverage to be biased? Is there even a chance that it will be biased?

The proof of the pudding is in the eating, and I think that, in the past, bit-tech's readers have found factual coverage from the show to be both positive and negative. The first event I attended had mixed coverage, and that, I believed, proved to the readers that such coverage was informative and independent. I have never had a single reader complain to me that my coverage of Intel was biased by my location reporting. If readers are happy, I'm happy. The flipside is that some people believe this to be so heinous a crime they would not contemplate it. Jason Calacanis, who used to run publications including Engadget, is a staunch believer in the declining of all such 'junkets'. "I'd rather fly economy on my own dime than fly business and accept a junket," he was once quoted as saying. Engadget readers, he reasons, won't stand for it. Even staunch defenders of editorial integrity - such as 'old school' hack Mike Magee, of TheRegister.com and TheInquirer.net, or even John C Dvorak, crank extraordinaire, are still happy to accept trips, despite their cutthroat approach to integrity. "Why should I have to bloody pay," Mike once told me over a beer, "To cover their bloody products, to be sat in a room and brainwashed by PR people for hours? If they want to try and brainwash me, they can bloody pay for me to bloody be there." A fair point.

So what's the basic conclusion? If you are a journalist that is lucky enough to have an unlimited budget for travel, you are probably better off travelling on your own dime to avoid entirely the question of independence. But most readers understand that no budget is unlimited, and are happy to see a journalist taken to an event if it gets them information they wouldn't otherwise have. The flipside for this indulgence is that, as a journalist, you'd better not screw those readers over with biased coverage – because if you do, they won't forgive you. Slamming a competitor Quite apart from the general ungentlemanliness of taking a pop shot at a competitor, to do so is generally considered bad form in the press - except, ironically, when you get to the higher echelons of reporting. If you think the blogosphere is bad, try looking at national newspapers. Owners of big nationals - such as The Guardian and the Daily Mail here in the UK - regularly use editorial to take a pop at each other's publications, reporting downward circulations, or story controversies.

Below the belt? Probably, but readers don't seem to mind. Who doesn't like a good mudslinging match? (For further insight online, see Nick Denton v Jason Calacanis, which has provided an industry with well-publicised fun for years now). What's also interesting to note is that this kind of trashing does actually go on all the time. Given the widespread interest of so many media moguls, competitor trashing and suppressing of bad information about your own company happens all the time it's just that most audiences don't always care or don't know it's going on. It's the reason that magazines like Private Eye exist - to keep the press honest and show up their blemishes. A prime example of this behaviour in the online world is the Wired and Digg controversy, which I mentioned earlier. Should Wired by writing about Digg when its parent company owns a competitor to Digg? This is where the issue of scale starts to come in. When you get into the mainstream media, into the big leagues, you generally find that a few people own almost everything.

You can make an argument, in many reporting jobs, that almost anything you write about will have a competitor from the parent company of your parent company. How much media and business does News Corporation own? Time Warner?

The issue comes down to credibility and readership expectation. Do I expect The Sun to disclose every time they write about a product or issue in which Rupert Murdoch has an interest? No, because half the newspaper would be filled with disclosures of Murdoch's interests, so I take it for granted. Do I expect Wired to disclose the interests of Conde Naste? This is borderline – Conde Naste clearly has a large portfolio of properties, but it's not exactly on the scale of News Corp. But in this case, I probably do.

Let's refine that. I don't believe that any writer on Wired actually has an interest in promoting Reddit - it's just another product in Conde's portfolio. I don't believe that any writer on Wired has any interest in trashing Digg, beyond creating a controversy that garners a cheap readership. But the fact that I can see that the topics are so related, in many ways, mandates disclosure, and this is a good rule. If you think your readership is going to query it, disclose it. This is often the rule that I come back to when thinking about this topic. In the Wired case, then, I expect disclosure - but I don't really think that it will affect the article per se.

TechCrunch has been on the receiving end of this stick, too. TechCrunch UK slammed a conference it was attending, Le Web 3, and promptly announced that it would be setting up its own conference in competition.

This is clearly a breach of what most people would recognise as journalistic ethics – there's no issue of scale here, since both companies involved are small enough to be intimately involved in each other's business. Trashing a show then announcing that you're setting up a competitor should send alarm bells ringing in most reader's heads. TechCrunch owner Mike Arrington was so annoyed at the actions of his staff in this editorial matter that he fired the Editor on the spot. Interesting stuff. Sponsorship, Advertising, Disclosing Interests This is something that comes up a lot partly because, as I mentioned above, many bloggers count themselves as journalists, ad sales guys and publishers all rolled into one.

At what point should you disclose interests and the business activities of your publication? Here's an easy one - The ScobleShow on PodTech. This is heavily, and clearly, sponsored by Seagate. I don't believe that a piece Robert Scoble does on Intel is going to be affected by his sponsorship by Seagate. Do I care if Seagate flies him somewhere to cover an event? Not really, since I'm guessing that's partly the point of his sponsorship.

I understand that Seagate is paying PodTech which is paying Scoble, and that's fine – that's how the publishing business works. But do I care about it when Scoble is talking about hard drives, or about Seagate? You bet I do, since I don't believe that there's anything like a Chinese Wall between PodTech's business staff and Scoble, not to mention the fact that I'm sure Scoble has a degree of a stake in his show's financial success. I don't believe that Scoble is going to be able to cover Seagate or its competitors without some degree of bias, conscious or unconscious, since my knowledge of Scoble, from watching his shows, is that he is massively grateful for the opportunities that the Seagate sponsorship gives him.

Now that's a mark of his enthusiasm and personality, which are good things. But they make him an unreliable journalist when it comes to covering these topics independently. That's OK, though, because I'm not watching Scoble to get anything purporting to be objective editorial. I'm watching because I want his personality and his take on things. So, as a viewer, I don't want disclosure all over the place, just where it's relevant. Let's take another one, and I'm going to call Tom Foremski out here. In a recent piece, Tom wrote about a company being run by a guy that he used to work with in some abstract capacity, and felt the need to disclose that in the middle of the piece. Meh. I don't really care - Foremski is an old-school hack, one of the best, and I don't believe for one second that his opinion can be bought. Besides, most journalists have friends throughout the industry they work in – just as everybody has friends at work. I don't believe that I need to know every time Foremski has lunch with a guy he used to know that now works somewhere else. We've talked about commercial interests acting to the detriment of editorial on the web, but it's interesting to note the degree to which we are happy to put up with commercial activity offline.

Advertorials are common in print magazines - how often do you see 'Special Advertising Feature' in glossy lifestyle magazines, where the entire 4 page spread has been paid for by a company? Many journalists consider these features the spawn of the business devil, but most readers probably don't care too much, especially in the sector they're often operating in. Most 16 year old girls don't care if a feature on makeup was sponsored by Max Factor, it's just not a big deal. Advertorials, on the other hand, have really not made their way onto the net in any significant way, and this actually puts most web publications ahead of mainstream mags in this respect.

I do believe that, when you start to get to more serious stuff, to bigger publications, that the Chinese Wall of commercial and editorial starts to get important. On bit-tech, the team writes a lot of product reviews, a lot of news, often covering the people that buy adverts in the banner slots around the site. If I was a reader, I would want to know that these reviews were unbiased. That's why we used to make a lot of the fact that we operated like a traditional magazine - the site has a rigid Chinese Wall, where editorial staff have no idea about the business deals that are being done.

Most of the time, we didn't even know who was buying space on the site until we saw their banner pop up as we viewed it. When I find a site like bit-tech, providing a lot of objective reviews of products, and it turns out that the site owner is the one selling the ads - I'm apprehensive. Sites like TechCrunch, PerezHilton - I'm happy for Mike and Perez to sell the ads there, because every day I'm reading their opinion, their thoughts, not reviews that are purporting to be 100% objective views of how I should be spending my money.

So when I see reviews, when I see products, I generally want the objectivity guaranteed by a Chinese wall. But that's just me. Free kit, NDAs Here's another one, and it's close to my heart - kit and disclosure agreements.

Many journalists e review an awful lot of kit, and many do sign non disclosure agreements. Views vary on how ethical this is, and how this compromises independence. Readers often used to ask us why we didn't buy every piece of hardware that we reviewed on bit-tech to avoid the pressure of manufacturers. 99% of our reviews were (and still are, to my knowledge) of products that were sent in to us by companies for review, and when we're done with the review they go back to the company afterwards.

Not having to deal with the company, readers would say, would mean that our reviews would be even more trustworthy. This is perhaps true, but it is also very impractical. We reviewed tens of thousands of pounds worth of kit every month. We could not afford to buy that, full stop. We'd have to up our advertising sales by a large factor, and that would result in a detriment to the layout and the look of a site, and this would be bad for the reader.

Quite apart from this, we'd never get to see hardware that was 'pre-release', never get to test hardware before it got on the shelves, as we often were able to.

Getting kit before it comes out, getting information to publish, is one of the key things that bit-tech does, and many review publications and news publications across every sector also rely on this stream of exclusive kit and articles to keep readers interested, whether it's a car launch or a hotel launch. To manage the relationship with companies, many publications sign non-disclosure agreements. Under these agreements, journalists agree not to write about a product until the company says it's OK - known as the 'embargo lift' - and in return, the journalist gets advanced, full access to the product, and often the engineers, designers etc behind it. What are the pros and cons of this? Well, signing an NDA means that when the product goes public, a journalist will know the necessary details to provide a reader with the kind of information the reader's going to want.

However, the downside is that, in the meantime, they can't write about the product, whereas others who don't sign the NDA will be able to - although they will invariably lack the same kind of access. Where you fall on this will often depend on the kind of publication you are.

The Inquirer is famous for not signing NDAs. Mike runs a news publication, and it operates primarily on scoops and exclusive details. Signing NDAs would handcuff them and reduce their ability to report in the way they want to. In that respect, NDAs are a downer. Bit-tech operates primarily on in-depth reviews and articles. Signing NDAs are a crucial part of getting at this information. Invariably, it is a compromise - often we'd like to write about a product we'd seen, but agreed not to in order to secure a look at the finished thing. This is a judgement call - we believe that the final, in-depth, wellresearched article is worth more than a haphazard preview and, crucially - NDAs only ever effect timing, not content. We never did, and I'm sure the team there never will, sign any agreement that dictates what the content of our article should be, rather than just the timing. That clearly does not serve the reader's interests, whereas we believe that signing NDAs related to timing often does, given the access and information it secures us. I will draw a quick further example from automotive journalism.

Most 'A-list' car journalists don't even own cars - they have a different model each week arrive on their doorstep and the keys posted through the letterbox. Does this affect their opinion of the car? I don't believe that it does, for the most part, because 'bribery' and a compromise of ethics requires going beyond the ordinary. I once spoke to a very senior car journalist who, when questioned about the role of review cars vis a vis independence, said - "There's no conflict. Nobody can bribe you, because everyone has to play by the same rules. Every company has to put their cars through the same process. As a Road Test Editor, I feel nothing towards the manufacturers that park these cars in my drive. It's just my job, and its just their job. Just because I get a car doesn't mean I review it well. I review cars badly all the time. And companies still have to send more cars, because, what, are they not going to ever have reviews?" The power struggle And this neatly brings me to, and illustrates my final point, which is to note the power struggle that exists between the press and the industries that the press covers. From an editorial perspective, companies want journalists to cover their products.

They want the publicity, they want the review quotes, they want the public to be exposed to what it is they do. By the same token, journalists want readers to see what they write, because the more readers they have, the more powerful the publication becomes. But as much as companies want to pander to the press, they also realise that they hold some of the power cards, to a degree. If a company has a big product, or a big announcement, the balance of power could shift. Maybe a number of publications are offering to cut deals to get the exclusive. All of them are prepared, to some degree, to compromise their normal editorial principles to get the exclusive. Look at NewsWeek magazine – most companies would give their right arm to get coverage in it. But NewsWeek will often have coverage, months in advance, of a new Apple product that they sit on in order to get the exclusive and keep Apple happy. Most people wouldn't consider NewsWeek an unethical publication, but this is an example of how the power moves between journalists and companies. Not to mention the fact that, fundamentally, companies pay the bills – by advertising.

The press is, in a basic way, operating at the behest of the advertisers that pay the bills. Now granted, advertisers are looking to get to publications which have a big readership, and big readership is generally created by independent editorial. But you can see how the whole thing is a weird kind of symbiotic relationship where there's a lot of possibility for difference in opinion and divergent operation.

CONCLUSIONS

So I hope this provides some useful analysis of the issues at hand. One thing that I really think can be drawn from this is that there are no set rules as to what is right and wrong when it comes to publishing and journalism - what is right and wrong comes down to what you are presenting yourself as and what your readers expect. I don't expect PerezHilton to be a bastion of independent and objective reporting, and the site does not present itself as such. Consequently, I'm willing to accept a different type of editorial conduct than I would from a site that presents itself as providing unbiased, objective reviews of products or services. What I want to get across is that 'right', when it comes to editorial ethics, will depend on reader expectations. In this respect, its easy to think of a gold standard of editorial conduct in a given sector - such as technology reviews - but that standard will surely not apply in something completely different, such as gossip reporting.

The blogging world appears to favour transparency and values it above all else. This is possibly a good thing, given the convoluted business conditions in which blogs often exist. Transparency also leads to trust, and many 'new' brands in the media need to build up that level of trust with the readership. Bigger, older publications have the luxury of pre-established trust and are able to write and present info without having to disclose left right and centre. Indeed, you can argue that old-school codes of conduct are very anti-competitive. Let's return to our travel conundrum. For Publication C to decree that the only ethical way to report on Company A is to pay for Journalist B to fly out itself, it casts a negative light on any journalists, perhaps from Company D, that might accept the payment offer due to their relative size and resources – even when Journalist E from company D might provide far more interesting / 'better' coverage. Help to a publication to finance coverage might look unethical, but it could also help provide support to a publication that could, one day, rival the established players.

Which is the greater good? I want to draw one final conclusion, and this is a very British conclusion, and it is merely my personal belief. It is this - true journalistic integrity requires cynicism. It requires authority, and it requires a total lack of awe. Journalists and bloggers need to take what may seem fantastic to an average person and completely discount its worth beyond an opinion. So a car turns up on my doorstep. Big deal. It might still be a lemon. So I get to use a new bleeding-edge PC for a month. Whatever. It's probably a crock anyway, and there are another 10 coming next week. So Company A wants to fly me to China. China sucks, and Company A sucks even harder. (And you wonder why old-school journalists are jaded and arrogant? It's what keeps their integrity and makes them good at their job).

To an everyday person - and, crucially and consequently, to many 'new' writers who have come up through the informal quasi-journalistic world of the blogosphere - this kind of stuff is out of this world; and it results in biased coverage, which is why transparency and ethics are such a big deal in this new media world. But don't assume that there's a gold standard that every publication in the world must live up to. There's no objective right and wrong. Adjust your expectations of a publication accordingly. And if a publication doesn't live up to your expectations, ditch it. Others will do the same.

10

Putting Theory to Practice

There has been considerable debate over the proper place of journalism education within the academy. We argue that programmes which compromise between vocational training and a broader programme of study based in the liberal arts remain unsatisfactory because they put too much onus on students themselves to bridge the gap between theory and practice. Taking up James Carey's challenge to more precisely locate the object of study, we believe journalism education must begin from a view of journalism as an institutional practice of representation with its own historical, political, economic and cultural conditions of existence. This means that the journalism curriculum must not only equip students with a particular skill set and broad social knowledge, but must also show students how journalism participates in the production and circulation of meaning.

INTRODUCTION

The proper place of journalism education within the academy in North America has prompted a century-long debate between those who advocate a singular focus on vocational training and those who would have journalism students follow a much broader programme of study based in the liberal arts. While this debate has spawned a range of programmes that attempt to compromise between these two approaches, discussion continues as to whether these curricula offer a truly integrated and comprehensive approach to journalism education. As James W. Carey argues: 'Journalism is surrounded now by many more well-conceived and well-taught courses in history, law, ethics, and similar subjects. However, the central subject matter, journalism, has not been found, but merely displaced to the margin' (Carey, 2000: 14).

In other words, while these liberal arts courses may produce more well-rounded graduates, questions remain as to whether they actually bridge the gap between the academic and vocational elements of the programme and provide more insight into the social dimensions of journalism as a professional practice (Reese and Cohen, 2000). More recently, a heated debate has been conducted among Australian journalism and media scholars regarding the proper role of cultural studies in journalism education (Turner, 2000; Windschuttle, 2000). This article takes up Carey's concerns and proposes shifting the focal point for journalism education. The object of study we propose is not simply that which working journalists do, the product of which we read in our newspapers and watch on the evening news. Rather, like some of our Australian colleagues (Bacon, 1999; Turner, 2000), we advocate a more holistic approach which posits journalism as an institutional practice of representation with its own historical, political, economic and cultural conditions of existence.

What this means to the journalism curriculum is that students require not only a particular skill set and broad social knowledge, but they also need to understand how journalism participates in the production and circulation of meaning in our society. In developing this perspective, we draw heavily from the field of critical communication studies. That is, we see disciplines such as semiotics, ethnography, discourse analysis and the political economy of communication all having strong application in coming to grips with journalistic practice. Given the range of this field of scholarship, of course, it is unreasonable to expect aspiring journalists, particularly at the undergraduate level, to become communication scholars. Moreover, we recognize that calling for a convergence of media, communication and journalism studies is not entirely new. In both the United States and Canada, departments of journalism and mass communication have been intertwined for years – a relationship that has itself been the object of controversy. Nevertheless, we argue that critical communication theory offers means for both a better understanding of the professional dimensions of journalism, as well as a vehicle for overcoming the oft-cited 'theory/practice' gap that seems to plague many programmes (Reese and Cohen, 2000: 216–17; Stephens, 2000).

In the first instance, communication theory provides direct insight into the process of communication itself. It can show journalists how their craft is part and parcel of a much larger process of social communication and how the ideological choices inherent in news values and news production are necessarily grounded in larger sets of social power. Communication theory helps elucidate the social context in which journalists work, drawing attention to the particular historical, economic, political and cultural conditions which govern their practice. It can illustrate how such things as the organization of work routines and patterns of ownership impact on patterns of media representation, and how – following McLuhan – the medium of communication itself 'massages' the message (e.g. Tuchman, 1978; Hackett and Gruneau, 2000). At the same time, communication theory posits journalism as a practice of meaning production – what Robert A. Hackett and Yuezhi Zhao have called the 'regime of objectivity' – to illustrate how journalists are implicated in the production and reproduction of particular ideas and conceptions of the world (Hackett and Zhao, 1998). In other words, communication theory provides the essential 'why' to the more pragmatic 'how' of journalistic method.

It also can help journalists understand the consequences of their stories: how stories are picked up and used by competing social actors. Communication theory offers journalism education a solid theoretical foundation and a clear answer to the thorny question of why journalism education matters, without resorting to the too-often simplistic and functionalist liberal and libertarian theories of the press. Second, and perhaps most importantly, critical communication theory provides a key link between skills-based and liberal arts courses. To a considerable extent, communication theory is the application of the liberal arts and the social sciences to processes of communication and, as such, offers students conceptual tools with which to negotiate between the practical and more abstract elements of their studies. For instance, the study of media policy illustrates how the public policy process can have direct play on the range of perspectives in the public realm.

The study of political communication illustrates how the political process itself tends to diffract and diffuse political debate. And the political economy of communication demonstrates how the distribution of political and economic resources impacts upon the circulation of ideas in the public sphere. These insights help journalism students develop a conscious understanding of the praxis of their craft and the role they play in a society in which our experience of the world is increasingly mediated by communications organizations and media professionals. This perspective provides a somewhat different view on journalism and the process of social communication than traditional liberal arts courses. It places the process of communication at the centre of inquiry and, in so doing, provides journalism students with a better understanding of how their profession, and the skills it encompasses, are woven into the larger social fabric.

But while the debate over the structure of the journalism curriculum has come a long way in the last hundred years, exactly how far away from practical training journalism programmes should move remains a contentious subject (see Turner, 2000). If in some quarters the need is expressed for an even more critical dimension to media education in general and journalism studies in particular – that is, 'teaching more "why" in addition to "how" in professional courses' (AEJMC, 1996: 107) – there is also considerable resistance to such a shift within journalism schools themselves (Stephens, 2000).

THE PROBLEM INSIDE THE SCHOOLS

While, as Douglas Anderson points out, 'It is difficult – and hazardous – to generalize about the strengths and shortcomings of journalism–mass communication education because... [f]ew criticisms – or ringing endorsements... fit the entire field,' one of the major difficulties in reforming journalism education lies in the structure of journalism faculties (Anderson, 1997: 37).

Despite some interest in increasing the scope of journalism education, putting these ideas into practice at the level of news production is another matter entirely. As G. Stuart Adam noted over ten years ago, 'the academic and professional elements of journalism curriculum are like "two nations warring within the bosom of a single state" ' (Adam, 1988a: 9).

That is, journalism education is the servant of two masters. On the one hand, journalism educators seek to satisfy the demands of news organizations by providing a steady stream of graduates ready for the newsroom. On the other hand, journalism schools are asked to meet the standards of university administrators who perceive post-secondary education as something more than vocational training. In both the literature on journalism education and in the classroom, doing journalism and talking about journalism are typically considered two different things (Bovee, 1999: 185).

To a large part this dichotomy rests on differences in the training and backgrounds of journalism faculty. As Howard Tumber, Michael Bromley and Barbie Zelizer (2000: 5) note: 'Journalism is taught almost everywhere chiefly by current and former practitioners whose academic groundings rarely intersect with the media/communication/cultural studies constituency'. Those who have taken the time to hone professional skills rarely hold graduate degrees and, because of the time required to earn a PhD, those with advanced degrees are not often sufficiently familiar with the more practical demands of the craft (Bovee, 1999: 185). And, as Adam (1988a: 9) argues, too often in this dichotomy it is the more 'academic' courses

– those dealing with issues arising from the critical literature – that are 'downgraded' by both faculty and students 'and considered as extras'.

Like these other commentators, it is our experience that journalism is often taught principally as a craft, as a method, and that much of the journalism-focused curriculum in journalism and mass communication education is devoted to imparting key elements of this method. Students learn to recognize news through rote learning of news values. The ideas of objectivity and balance are deployed and embraced as simple narrative devices for developing perspective and point of view. Students develop a sense of style and narrative structure through learning how to write leads and different story forms – e.g. the feature, the profile, the court case. They also learn layout and copy-editing techniques, computer and Internet research skills, the operation of specific software programmes and, sometimes, basic photography skills. The emphasis remains on skills development to produce employable graduates who are ready to pull their weight in the time-constrained 'miracle' of industrial news production.

The problem is that much of this method is presented uncritically, as simply 'the way it is'. Students 'learn by doing' and serious study of the larger ideological dimensions of news values, story form and narrative structure, and the commercial influences on principles of layout and design, is rendered secondary to skills acquisition. What is missing from this craft-based approach is a clear understanding that news production is, in fact, the convergence of theory and practice, and that any attempt to provide fair, balanced and accurate depictions of events involves much more than a simple presentation of 'the facts'. This is tantamount to having a method that denies any relation to epistemology. Students are taught a way of seeing and presenting the world without fully understanding the reasons why they are employing a particular method or the impact that the tools they utilize have on the depictions they render. There is little understanding that their methods yield very particular ways of seeing, and ultimately, ways of knowing the world (Fishman, 1980: 134; Tuchman, 1978: 179). As the AEJMC Curriculum Task Force put it, this amounts to a separation of the 'how' and 'why' of journalism (AEJMC, 1996: 107).

DEVELOPING A CRITICAL EDGE

In an attempt to bridge this divide between what is sometimes called the 'theory' and 'practice' of journalism, a number of writers have proposed ways of incorporating more critical perspectives into journalism education. Some see the road to reform as simply supplementing the existing curriculum. Others argue for more radical measures.

Stephen D. Reese and Jeremy Cohen (2000: 214–22) argue that journalism scholarship requires a renewed independence to help academics resist domination by the demands of industry and the 'administrative research agenda' of mainstream US communication research.

They call for a 'strengthened professionalism' among journalism scholars, one which includes multiple 'points of engagement with journalism and media professionals' while remaining alert to a university's obligation 'to prepare students not only to be employed but also to participate effectively and critically in the democratic community'. However, Reese and Cohen also point out that critical and cultural studies – research which incorporates an analysis of power – 'do not typically engage much with the professions and are easily marginalized' because of the 'theory/ practice' gap (Reese and Cohen, 2000: 220). Peter Parisi advocates an integrated curriculum, but rather than a liberal arts emphasis, he maintains that 'critical, cultural, or qualitative studies provide clearer focus and greater coherence for journalism education'. As he sees it, such an approach would treat journalism as a site of public discourse and foreground the question of epistemology, examining journalistic storytelling 'as a specific rhetorical form, not a transparent stenography of the real'. Parisi contends, for instance, that practising journalists employ a facile theory of knowledge based largely on interviews with sources. 'In journalism, the gathering and description of "truth" is straightforward and, philosophically if not practically, unproblematic. Journalism treats facts as simple things.'

Such a theory of knowledge, of course, ignores a whole body of contemporary thought in the social sciences. Parisi writes: 'Truth is not "found" but is defined by the very methodologies, languages, technologies, cultural assumptions, economic imperatives, and literary systems through which it is sought and represented. For liberal study, facts, knowledge and truth are not "out there" but are socially constructed' (Parisi, 1992: 5–7). Mark Fishman, in a widely cited study of the social construction of news, uses the example of a crime wave to illustrate this point: 'a crime wave is little more than a theme in crime (e.g. crime against the elderly, crime in the subways) that is heavily and continuously reported'. By using the particular news theme of a crime wave, news organizations have an organizing concept that allows them to view disparate incidents as somehow related. 'News organizations created the wave, not in the sense that they invented crimes, but in the sense that they gave a determinant form of content to all incidents they reported.' (Fishman, 1980: 5–11). Dennis M. Wilkins, too, insists that journalism education include theoretical and methodological grounding.

In science, evidence stems from ongoing verification; in journalism, evidence consists of information from sources whose reliability often is dependent solely on their availability. That information may be verified, but only in the sense of obtaining independent verification that what the first source said is correct, not necessarily that it is true or valid. (Wilkins, 1998: 70)

In journalism, assertions are reported as if they were true, whether or not they have been grounded in a rigorous process of verification. In fact, the presupposition is such a basic component of all journalism that it extends to both so-called quality and tabloid reporting. A tabloid story is 'accurate' if it faithfully reports what was said or written by sources. By this standard much of what is written in tabloids can be claimed to be 'exceptionally accurate' – including, one might add, the testimony of experts on alien abductions (Bird, 1990: 378).

Wilkins's argument, then, is a call for a much more sophisticated understanding of what constitutes truth and fact than journalists are typically armed with. Working to find ways to incorporate such insights into the curriculum, Les Switzer, John McNamara and Michael Ryan recommend that journalism students study news texts, not as models to emulate, but as instances of mass communication as a 'powerful symbolic force'. News stories are not simple transcriptions of actuality but highly constructed treatments of reality. 'One should look for messages within news texts that appear to privilege certain cultural practices and denigrate, silence, or diminish other cultural practices'. Rather than take for granted the structure of news narratives, students should understand them as examples of the 'realistic narrative' form. 'This is a genre of story-telling associated with the making of various kinds of cultural texts, where information and ideas about people, events, or situations, past and present, are categorized, prioritized, and condensed into chronological accounts that claim authority and public currency, impute cause, and assert their own truths' (Switzer et al., 1999: 29–30). Other critics are more circumspect in embracing change and argue that while more critical perspectives may have a place in journalism education, emphasis on the practical elements of the curriculum must be secured so that journalism does not become simply a 'species of the social sciences'.

As Warren G. Bovee argues, 'journalism scholars are heavily devoted to the social sciences approach in their graduate studies' and sometimes tend to cast 'journalism programmes in this mold'. Consequently, 'the concept of journalism as a profession – which identifies journalism as primarily practical work rather than as an object of study – suffers a fatal blow' (Bovee, 1999: 186). From this perspective, while reform might be necessary, it must keep the practice of journalism at the centre of the curriculum. Jay Rosen and Davis Merritt, the principal proponents of public or civic journalism, have championed the need to bring theory and practice closer together (Rosen, 1998, 1999; Merritt, 1995). Rosen and Merritt advocate self-reflexivity among reporters. They ask reporters to question their role as impartial presenters of facts and to understand how facts are 'made to mean' through the deployment of narrative structures. Moreover, public journalism asks reporters to take seriously their role as facilitators of critical public opinion in order that they may strive to make public life 'go well'.

Clearly, however, the aim of developing a more critical curriculum should not be to undermine the practical elements of journalism education. Rather, the point is to enhance students' understanding of their professional practice, encourage them to develop more incisive powers of observation and description and give them a sense of the power they wield. G. Stuart Adam offers one of the most comprehensive models for this kind of reform. As he sees it, journalism education's association with the social sciences has caused the fragmentation of the journalism curriculum into a set of discontinuous fields, namely professional practices, ethics, communications and society, communication theory, communication law, and so on. While these categories of interest and knowledge are sound, they are not linked in a manner which makes them seem like elements in a single body of knowledge. They seem to have an independence, one from another, connected neither by method nor object of enquiry. (Adam, 1988b: 77)

Consequently, he argues that these disparate components of journalism education should be reorganized into 'a single field of Journalism Studies... just as political science represents an integration of separate approaches into the single subject of politics'. In turn, 'with journalism as the unambiguous point of reference, the field should then be divided into five sub-fields'. The first is what he calls the philosophy of journalism, which includes the history of the idea of freedom of expression, the moral claims of journalists, the 'meaning' of journalistic work and analysis of journalism's intentions and goals. The second is the range of professional practices and methods journalists employ. These would include newsgathering, writing, editing, layout and design, and radio, television and film techniques. Adam's third sub-field is social and political context.

This field 'locates communications systems in the landscape of power, social structure, culture and behaviour'. The fourth is criticism, which he defines as 'thoughtful reflections on the moral, technical, intellectual and artistic achievements of journalists'. Finally, Adam proposes a sub-field of methodology, consisting of 'the self-conscious development and evaluation of the methods by which we create knowledge'. He writes: 'Journalism Studies is a branch of the humanities and the social sciences and shares with them the methodological dilemmas, curiosities and disputes of the other disciplines' (Adam, 1988b: 77–8).

Whether or not one agrees with the specific prescriptions of these writers, their recognition that the curriculum needs to bridge the divide between the theoretical and practical elements of traditional journalism education is a welcome intervention to the debate. Without an understanding of how the practice of journalism impinges on the way in which ideas and events are represented, the liberal arts component of programmes loses much of its force. Simply putting skills-based training and liberal arts courses side-by-side doesn't show students how to apply those ideas and concerns in the context of social communication in general and journalism in particular. If anything, it reinforces the idea that the liberal arts have no practical application and do not inform the journalistic method. We reject this separation of theory and practice.

INTEGRATING THE CURRICULUM

Rather than undertake a wholesale restructuring of the curriculum, we advocate using some of these ideas to help draw common ground between the academic and vocational elements of journalism education. Two important steps in this direction involve: (1) re-orienting course curriculum such that the courses have common themes or elements running through them; and (2) taking administrative measures to help heal the apparent division between theory and practice within journalism schools. In this process, the challenges are to remind students that journalism is a complex process of re-presentation and to promote a more rigorous notion of journalism as an object of study among both students and faculty.

To begin building common ground between different elements of the curriculum and help instil a more critical and self-reflexive bent in journalism education, we would like to demonstrate how three themes common to critical communication studies have practical application to courses in which the method of journalism is taught. These themes can be introduced to applied courses, such as writing and reporting workshops, and to more academic courses, such as those in history, ethics, media law and contemporary media issues. The purpose is to alter the reference point in curriculum development, to refuse to accept journalism as simple technique and, instead, emphasize that journalism is a complex professional practice that involves the application of key vocational skills as well as a critical analytic eye.

JOURNALISM AS A PRACTICE OF MEANING PRODUCTION

Any number of the courses we teach, writing workshops as well as courses that investigate contemporary issues in journalism, provide us with an opening to posit journalism as a practice of meaning production. Journalists do not simply 'find' meaning in the raw data – 'the facts', interviews, etc. – they use to write stories. Rather, they create meaning out of, or from, this information. As Robert Karl Manoff (1987: 228) puts it: 'News occurs at the conjunction of events and texts, and while events create the story, the story also creates the event.' From choosing to cover one event over another, to the choice of language used in a story, to where the story is finally placed in the newspaper or programme line-up, news production is a complex process of selection through which journalists produce meaning. In the words of Switzer et al. (1999: 28): 'The power of news texts... lies in the power to confer meaning on persons, events, or issues'. Peter Parisi adds:

> From a critical/cultural studies perspective, news writing represents a set of choices: choices that (a) define an issue as newsworthy and certain questions as relevant; (b) admit, mute, or reject information, sources, and perspectives; and (c) decide the level and extent of detail and 'color' with which to render a person, community, region, or issue. (1992: 8)

Because journalists employ words and images as tools within a system of representation, it is fundamental that students understand the signifying power of language, that they have some understanding of Saussurean linguistics and the relationship between the signifier and the signified, a relationship in which they are implicated every time they report. Students need to understand that the choices they make in taking their notes, in choosing who to interview, in deciding what line of questioning to pursue and, ultimately, in choosing what material from their notebooks to include in their stories, have a significant impact on the story they tell. Simple words like 'family' and 'spouse' serve as illustrative examples of how politically charged the use of commonplace words can be. Does 'family' mean nuclear family, extended family, single-parent family? Can it include same-sex parents? These distinctions are extremely relevant when the story pertains to residential zoning regulations, immigration or child-care benefits.

Does 'spouse' imply a relationship based on a legally sanctioned heterosexual marriage, or does the term include common-law partners and same-sex relationships? These meanings are pertinent to stories about the institution of marriage, inheritance laws and pension regulations. Similarly, the adjectives, nouns, verbs and adverbs journalists employ in their coverage attribute more precise meanings to the event. Is the group of people demonstrating outside the corporate headquarters a 'mob', a 'crowd', an 'army' or a 'cluster', each of which connotes a slightly different kind of group? While to some extent the ideological nature of these choices may seem self-evident, it is our experience that such close study of these representational tools engenders in students a sense of responsibility for the language they use and the archival material they gather to help them write stories. It also helps students understand that news stories are constitutively linked to political struggles and that journalism is not simply 'a transparent stenography of the real' but that it is implicated in creating and circulating shared social meanings and understandings of the world. Such an approach to journalism education also invites consideration of the institutional context of journalism, and particularly the political economy of news production. Citing media economist Robert Picard, Parisi notes:

> Typically, students hear uncritical presentations of a mythology of journalism, including 'the concept of citizen participation in democratic societies, the marketplace of ideas, free press' all leading to 'the coalescent myth that a free press is equivalent to commercial, profit-oriented journalism and that capitalist media systems offer the best option for free flow of ideas. (Parisi, 1992: 9)3

In our experience, too often the context in which journalism is practised has been naturalized as commercial enterprise, and too often the myth that there has traditionally been a 'firewall' between the editorial and commercial sides of the business leaves unexplored the ways in which the news values journalists deploy, the organizational work routines, the structure and layout of news publications and programmes, and the rhythms of news production are related to the commercial demands of their employers, especially in the more vocational or 'hands on' courses.

Instead, students should be set to critically questioning the ways in which a broader set of cultural, political and economic forces structure the practice of journalism. In this way, they might come to better identify – and work to overcome – the constraints the larger system places on their professional practice, as well as the systemic barriers to democratic performance.

JOURNALISM WITHIN ITS BROADER CULTURAL CONTEXT

Similarly, any number of courses we teach offer the opportunity to cast journalism within its broader cultural context – that is, to lay bare the stereotypical characterizations that so often pervade conventional reporting. Any news story, if it is to be understood by a majority of the members of civil society, must contain common narrative structures which help make possible the intersubjectivity required for deliberative politics. Reporters do not have unlimited time and space to tell their stories and explain what are sometimes extremely complex situations. Consequently, both journalists and audiences bring narrative structures or 'news frames' to particular events to help interpret them and give them meaning. As Todd Gitlin (1980: 6, 49) writes, such frames are important because they are 'composed of little tacit theories about what exists, what happens, and what matters' and they tend to reject or downplay 'material that is discrepant'. It is particularly important for students to avoid stereotypical narratives and news frames when observing, interacting with, and describing cultures, subcultures, communities and religions to which they don't belong and about which they may have very limited knowledge and experience (which, these days could well be much of the time).

Whether our students become foreign correspondents, beat reporters or general assignment reporters, they will have to learn how to deal responsibly in their work with the alternative values, belief systems, social systems, traditions and histories of the people they write about, whether those people are Kosovar refugees, squeegie kids or professional musicians. Consequently, while all three of the curricular elements discussed here are inflected with ethnography, some familiarity with the ethnographic method is particularly important if one is to write and report about other cultures and subcultures with a sense of fairmindedness and responsibility. Students need to learn to let subjects and events 'speak for themselves', rather than slot them into predefined social roles. To recognize how pervasive this problem is, we need only think about the stereotypes we regularly encounter in the news media, stereotypes of Muslims, feminists, professional athletes, native peoples, welfare recipients, even university professors. These stereotypes continue to be produced and reproduced by working journalists. In part this is due to time and space constraints faced by journalists. In the face of these constraints they rely upon well-known narratives. But these 'misrepresentations' are also the product of the fact that they are ill equipped to reflect on their practice.

Perhaps the best illustration of this is the kind of coverage of Islam that we see from Canadian and American news organizations. Reportage of the crash of Egypt Air Flight 990 in the fall of 1999 raised serious epistemological and ethnographic questions by leaping to sensational conclusions about a suicidal pilot in the face of scant and confusing evidence, conclusions that were only plausible in the context or frame of the hundreds of other news stories we have read about 'crazed Islamic terrorists'. Similarly, coverage of Algerians crossing the Canadian border into Vermont and Washington state in December 1999 led to wild speculative stories which again relied on flimsy evidence and which ran way ahead of complex investigations by law-enforcement officials on both sides of the international border.4 Edward Said assigns journalists an 'intellectual responsibility' for the depictions they produce. He writes:

> ... all knowledge is interpretation, and that interpretation must be self-conscious in its methods and its aims if it is to be vigilant and humane, if it is also to arrive at knowledge. But underlying every interpretation of other cultures... is the choice facing the individual scholar or intellectual: whether to put intellect at the service of power or at the service of criticism, community, dialogue, and moral sense. (Said, 1997: 170–2)

Part of this intellectual responsibility is a more sophisticated grasp of the journalistic method, even invoking the scientific methods of knowledge production that Wilkins (1998) recommends. After all, as G. Stuart Adam reminds us: 'Reporting is to journalism as research and evidence-gathering is to scholarship' (Adam, 1988b: 74). Whether we are teaching courses in international journalism, contemporary media issues, or writing and reporting workshops, we have the opportunity to raise, and introduce students to, ethnographic issues.

JOURNALISM AS A PRACTICE OF KNOWLEDGE PRODUCTION

Finally, any number of standard courses in the journalism curriculum could be used to foreground the notion of journalism as a practice of knowledge production. Earlier, we suggested that journalism students be aware of the practice of meaning production, by which we meant the different ways in which news texts themselves can be expressive. The practice of knowledge production is related to these concerns, but by using this phrase we wish to draw attention to the tests of rigour and verification applied by reporters. What we are proposing here is a different way into the topic, a way which foregrounds epistemological questions. Students and journalism educators, that is, need to consider where knowledge comes from, how it is produced in the process of news production. This topic seems especially applicable to courses which teach journalism's favoured research method: interviewing. In this context, we need to consider not only who to interview and how to interview, but also why to interview. In other words, we need to think about what we, as journalists, are seeking from the interview. Why are we interviewing who we are interviewing? Are we helping create a new or better understanding of the situation or simply playing upon stereotypes and accelerating the spin of PR campaigns?

Typically interviews are discussed in journalism classes, as well as in newsrooms, as sources of opinion, perspective and commentary, not to mention lively quotations. But this material, while essential, constitutes a very limited approach to the subject, and has more to do with stenography – he said, she said – than with journalism. Interviews offer the opportunity to engage with power, to confront establishment thinkers with the ramifications, the contradictions, even the sophistry of their public pronouncements. They provide an opportunity to challenge the people who produce and reproduce conventional wisdom. From this perspective, interviews are much more than sources of quotes, they are sites where public knowledge is produced and conventional interpretations are open to contestation. This is not to advocate that journalists become debating partners with their interview subjects.

But it does insist that journalists become more than uncritical recorders. It means asking challenging questions, it means giving some thought to how the people they interview know what they claim to know, to consider the expertise of their interview subjects and the bounds to that expertise. By all means, journalists are obliged to ask politicians about child poverty and business leaders about unemployment, but journalists are also obliged to evaluate the grounds upon which the answers to those questions are based. A particularly good example of this kind of interviewing can be seen in an article by Ken Auletta, who conducted a series of interviews for The New Yorker with some of the most powerful people in the American film and television industry, people like Rupert Murdoch, Oliver Stone, Michael Eisner, Deborah Winger, Steven Seagal, Michael Ovitz and David Geffen (Auletta, 1997).

In an attempt to understand the values of those who produce the sex and violence we see on our screens, Auletta asked each of them: 'What Won't You Do?' A number of interviewing techniques distinguish Auletta's work. First and foremost, the article is not about these people as celebrities, but about the programming decisions they make and the serious social issues those decisions inform. Second, Auletta knows what he is talking about. He responds to Rupert Murdoch's vague and abstract responses with specific examples and 'for instances', drawing out more substantive comments (Auletta, 1997: 70–3). He challenges Oliver Stone and Michael Eisner when they equate criticism with censorship (pp. 75–8). He repeats questions to cut off evasive answers from Michael Ovitz (pp. 86–7). Third, Auletta's knowledge base allows him to assert control over the interview because he demonstrates a much better command of his material than any of his interview subjects, thereby combatting the sensation of intimidation an interviewer might feel in the presence of such powerful individuals. Ultimately, he exposes frequent contradictions between their words about sex and violence on the screen, and their actions as programmers. In this way Auletta undermines their discursive power, turning the interviews into a highly informative dialogue in which the journalist participates actively in the production of knowledge. He does it with such skill that the focus of the story remains film and television programming, rather than Auletta himself or any of the stars with which he engages. The limited resources and time allotted to reporters by today's leaner newsrooms obviously circumscribes the kind of in-depth reporting we are advocating here. But a renewed commitment on the part of journalism scholars to insist on rigorous challenges to power could provide much-needed resistance from within the culture of journalism itself.

CHANGE AT THE INSTITUTIONAL LEVEL

Instituting the development of a critical praxis involves several dimensions. On the administrative side, tenure committees, university administrators, and even the industry, should acknowledge the need for forms of professional development that will allow faculty members with diverse backgrounds – e.g. practitioners and academics – to familiarize themselves with each other's kinds of expertise. When faculty members have diverse, even antagonistic backgrounds, a critical praxis is difficult to achieve.

Inside programmes, curriculum needs to be more flexible as well. In our experience, while programme-based publications sometimes let students experiment with style and form, the pressure to build clipping files and portfolios that can be used to woo potential employers drives students to emulate work found in the mainstream media – warts and all.

Students, instead, need to explore writing from different cultural perspectives, to experiment with different ways of framing events while in school. If they do not have practice deploying these principles in the context of their studies, they will find it all but impossible when they leave. This approach is already being encouraged by like-minded journalism educators in Australia (see Bacon, 1999). Similarly, skills building exercises should be incorporated into all elements of the curriculum, including liberal arts courses. Writing, interviewing, and computer skills are key to a journalist's success. Moreover, the emergence of the Internet as both a research tool and as a news medium in its own right has added to the menu of basic training students require. Consequently, students can be encouraged to experiment with different story and writing forms.

They can write editorials and feature articles instead of traditional essays and research papers, and they can be encouraged to use interviews, rather than books and articles, as the primary sources for their work. Faculties at universities and colleges often represent a range of perspectives and ideas that are excluded from mainstream journalism and students can be encouraged to seek out and use these unconventional sources in their work. Similarly, in the more academic courses, students should be encouraged to utilize 'workplace' technologies and software in their research and writing, and to illustrate their work with photographs, charts and graphs. While arranging and marking these kinds of assignments can mean more work for administrators and instructors, they can certainly help break down divisions between faculty members and pay off for students. Finally, the traditionally close relationship between journalism schools and the private, profit-driven news industry needs to be addressed. The success of any journalism programme is generally measured by the number of internship opportunities it affords and the kinds of jobs graduates are able to land.

A good placement record – meaning permanent employment in prestigious media outlets – attracts favourable programme reviews and strong student applications. Indeed, many students turn to journalism education because it provides 'practical' training and job opportunities. However, media owners and managers do not generally welcome critical perspectives on media practices, particularly those that might impact negatively on the bottom line (Hackett and Gruneau, 2000: 67–9). 'Thus,' as Hanno Hardt argues, 'any recognition by media organizations of particular educational institutions as certified sites of professional instruction reinforces an alliance with media interests rather than with the needs and interests of journalists' (Hardt, 1998: 210).

Moreover, in the present climate the traditional distances between editorial and commercial elements of news production are collapsing, even disappearing. As Neil Henry (1999: 69) observes, this weakening of the 'traditional "firewall" between the often-conflicting interests of the newsroom and the business and advertising departments' has eroded traditional journalism standards and rendered criticism of editorial quality even less welcome than they have historically been. A conscientious journalism educator working in such a climate has to be careful, as Will Straw remarked some years ago, not to measure 'pedagogical success by one's ability to render students professionally unemployable' (Straw, 1985: 7). To help loosen the hold industry imperatives exert on curriculum design, measures of programme success that do not depend on such close ties with the mainstream media need to be developed and promoted. The skill set learned in journalism schools has increasingly wide application, and stretching the scope of opportunity for graduating students would relieve some of the industry pressure to cater to narrow corporate concerns.

More emphasis could be placed on freelance opportunities and skills for starting alternative publications, which would help students create their own opportunities and overcome the corporate division of labour that permits managers control over content. While the increased concentration of ownership is shrinking opportunities for journalism graduates in the mainstream press (Henry, 1999), there is room for the growing number of journalism graduates entering the labor market to ply their trade on the Internet and in exploding specialty markets –e.g. trade magazines, in-house publications, all-news radio stations, specialty TV channels.

CONCLUSION

The point of a critical approach to journalism education is to redefine the object of study, to move away from 'journalism as it is practiced' to the framing of journalism as an institutional practice of representation with its own historical, political, economic and cultural conditions of existence. While this reformulation of journalism school remains contentious, and the steps involved in its actualization are complex, the introduction of critical communication studies to the journalism curriculum offers students a means of bridging the practical and abstract components of course work and provides journalism as a method with a sound epistemological basis.

Finally, journalism educators must themselves strive to be self-reflexive. As Hanno Hardt (1992: 9) writes: 'There is... a relatedness of history to theory that is constituted in the relationship between theorists and their cultural environment. Theories are the product of historical practice within a cultural setting; they emerge from such environments as contemporary explanations of society'. As journalism educators, we should reflect upon the extent to which the curriculum is a product of such larger social and political conditions. Walter Lippmann's (1922) prescription, for example, that reporters should translate the knowledge acquired by an educated elite to society at large, was born out of a fear, prevalent in the 1920s, that atomized individuals living in mass societies were easily susceptible to suggestion and, therefore, illequipped for participation in democracy.

Few journalism educators hold such opinions today (at least openly) and yet, today's sourcing routines are, in part, a result of Lippmann's considerable influence. Reflexivity is a difficult, fallible, but necessary component of journalism training if underlying assumptions concerning journalism's place in society are not to become hypostatized and taken for granted as common sense. If reporters are to practice their craft in a creative and energetic fashion they must first understand the potential fetters to their work; they cannot simply learn, by rote, the prescribed skills and tropes of storytelling. 'To work in the world,' Zygmunt Bauman suggests, '(as distinct from being "worked out and about" by it) one needs to know how the world works' (Bauman, 2000: 86). We are arguing for a journalism curriculum that is committed to explaining the historically contingent status of journalism; and, in so doing, we are hopeful that such a curriculum may help open doors to the possible.

While over the years the numbers have varied, the ACEJMC has recommended that at least 75 percent of the curriculum be composed of liberal arts courses (AEJMC, 1996). Nevertheless, public journalism's reflexivity has limits. It does not extend to questioning the role of the market. The goals and interests of profit-oriented news organizations are considered to be largely compatible with the goals of public journalism, and to the extent that they are not, it assumes, uncritically, that these conflicts can be overcome by the principled work of committed public journalists. For an extensive critique of public journalism, see Compton (2000). J. Herbert Altschull makes similar observations. He damns US journalism schools as 'essentially training grounds in the capitalist ideology of the press'.

This ideology, Altschull contends, comprises 'four articles of faith': that the press is free from the outside interference of the state, advertisers and the public; that the press serves 'the public's right to know;' that the press seeks to learn and disseminate the truth; and that the press reports facts objectively and fairly (Altschull, 1984: 114–18). Blindly accepting such 'articles of faith' serves to elide the larger social context of journalism and direct attention away from consideration of its larger structural determinants. For examples of coverage, see Phillips and Harris (1999), MacKenzie (2000) and Van Praet (2000). The University of British Columbia's Sing Tao School of Journalism found itself embroiled in a controversy over its corporate-media benefactor prior to opening its doors in 1998. Many members of the university's senate wanted the Sing Tao name stripped from the school. A recent graduate of the journalism programme at Concordia University in Montreal was offered a job with an espionage agency, the Canadian Security Intelligence Service. She was told that her fluency in three languages and the research and writing skills she acquired as a journalism student were ideal qualifications for an entry-level job.

Bibliography

Bliss, Edward: *Now the News: The Story of Broadcast Journalism,* New York, Columbia University Press, 1991.

Caswell, Lucy Shelton: *Guide to Sources in Sports Journalism History,* New York, Greenwood Press, 1989.

Crowley, David. J. and Paul Heyer: *Sports Journalism in History*, Boston, Allyn and Bacon, 2003.

De Wolk, Roland: *Introduction to Online Journalism*, Boston, Allyn & Bacon, 2001.

Ehrlich, Matthew C.: *Sports Journalism in the Movies*. Urbana: University of Illinois Press, 2004.

Ghiglione, Loren: *The American Journalist: Paradox of the Press,* Washington, Library of Congress, 1990.

Hudson, Frederick: *Journalism in the United States from 1690-1872*, New York, Routledge, 2000.

Kolodzy, Janet: *Convergence Journalism: Writing and Reporting Across the News Media*, Llanham, MD: Rowman & Littlefield, 2006.

Ness, Richard: *From Headline Hunter to Superman: A Journalism Filmography*, Landham, MD: Scarecrow Press, 1997.

Robert W. Snyder: *Defining Moments in Journalism*, New Brunswick, NJ: Transaction Publishers, 1998.

Ross, Lillian: *Reporting Back: Notes on Journalism*, Washington, DC: Counterpoint, 2002.

Sachsman, David B.: *The Civil War and the Press*, New Brunswick, NJ: Transaction Publishers, 2000.

Sims, Norman: *Literary Journalism in the Twentieth Century*, New York, Oxford University Press, 1990.

Index

□□□